ANGEL BC
London

Particles, Jottings, Sparks

Rabindranath Tagore was born in 1861, into one of the leading families of Calcutta; his father headed the Hindu reform movement the Brahmo Samaj. He had little formal schooling. He started writing and publishing verse at an early age; the first collected edition of his poems and dramas was published in 1896, and his frequent essays on cultural and political topics put him at the centre of contemporary debate. In 1912 he made his third visit to England, where his religious lyrics in his own English translations were admired by W.B. Yeats and published by Macmillan, leading to his winning the Nobel Prize for Literature in 1913. Thereafter for the rest of his life he was everywhere accorded the status of a prophet and guru. In the 1920s and '30s he undertook extended lecture tours of America, Europe and the Far East, the proceeds from which, like those from his publications in the West, went to Visva-Bharati, the school and international university he created at Santiniketan, north-east of Calcutta. In the last decade of his life he turned to painting on a prolific scale. He died in 1941, in the house in which he was born.

Tagore's vast and innovative achievement in almost all literary genres in verse and prose — only a small fraction of which has been successfully translated into English — makes him the leading figure in modern Indian literature. His compassionate wholeness of outlook, humanist and rationalist, as respectful of modern science as of India's spiritual heritage, has imparted a civilised ideal that has not been overturned.

William Radice is a poet, translator and scholar. He has published five books of his own poems. Among his translations from Bengali are *Selected Poems* and *Selected Short Stories* of Tagore (Penguin) and a version of Tagore's play *The Post Office*. He is Senior Lecturer in Bengali and Head of the Departments of South and South East Asia at the School of Oriental and African Studies, University of London.

RABINDRANATH TAGORE

Particles, Jottings, Sparks

The Collected Brief Poems

Translated with an Introduction by
William Radice

ANGEL BOOKS
London

First published in Great Britain 2001 by
Angel Books, 3 Kelross Road, London N5 2QS

1 3 5 7 9 10 8 6 4 2

British Library Cataloguing in Publication Data:
A catalogue record for this book is available from
the British Library

ISBN 0 946162 66 2

Typeset in Times New Roman by
Nikita Overseas Pvt Ltd
19A Ansari Road
New Delhi 110 002

Printed in India by
Gopsons Papers Ltd
A-14, Sector 60
Noida 201 301

To Martin Kämpchen

Da du du selbst bist ·
bin ich in deiner Schuld....

Contents

Preface

This book follows my earlier translations of Rabindranath Tagore for Penguin: *Selected Poems* (1985, rev. 1987) and *Selected Short Stories* (1991, rev. 1994). In those two books, selection was forced on me by the enormous size of Tagore's output. One can imagine, ultimately, a complete English translation of his short stories, but not of his poems or songs. It will therefore remain difficult for the non-Bengali reader to appreciate his *oeuvre* in its entirety.

By translating all three of his books of brief poems, however, I hope to show what he achieved in this particular genre. As with the earlier poems and the stories, I have also tried to set the translations in context by supplying an extensive introduction. There seemed no need for notes at the end; but in the Appendices I have translated some prose pieces that shed light on the poems' method and underlying thought. The book ends with two short texts given to me by a friend in Calcutta that have not — even in Bengali — been published before.

The translations are mine alone, but I have greatly benefited from careful and perceptive comments by Arun Deb of Konnagar

(*Particles* and *Jottings*), Maya Al-Farooq of the Südasien-Institut in Heidelberg (*Sparks*) and Gopa Majumdar of London (translations in the Introduction and Appendices).

Valuable comments from the English reader's point of view were made by Robert Goodwin, who has encouraged me in my work for over twenty years; and by my mother-in-law, Joy Stephenson.

I wrote the Introduction in February and March 1998 in Rabindra Bhavana, Santiniketan. I should like to thank the staff there for their help and kindness, the School of Oriental and African Studies for sabbatical leave, and the British Academy for the grant that made the visit possible.

I was inspired to translate Tagore's brief poems by Martin Kämpchen's German translations of a hundred of them in *Auf des Funkens Spitzen* (Kösel-Verlag, München, 1989; expanded to 120 in a new pocket-sized edition, 1997). In so many aspects of my work, Dr Kämpchen has been an unfailing mentor and friend, through correspondence and through meetings in Germany and Santiniketan. There are several people without whom this book would not have been completed, but without Martin-dā (as he is known to his many friends in Santiniketan and Ghosaldanga) I don't think I would have started it: hence its dedication, which quotes from his translation of *Sphuliṅga* 77 (No. 29 in the expanded edition of *Auf des Funkens Spitzen*).

Every existence has its idiom, every thing has an idiom and tongue,

He resolves all tongues into his own and bestows it upon men, and any man translates, and any man translates himself also,

One part does not counteract another part, he is the joiner, he sees how they join....

—*Walt Whitman*, 'Song of the Answerer'

Introduction

Master that he was of all poetic genres, Rabindranath Tagore is said to have been asked at times, 'Why haven't you written an epic?' There are several answers he could have given. He could have said that he did not think he could match up to the great classical epics of India, the *Mahābhārata* and *Rāmāyaṇa*. Or he could have said that modern Bengali literature already had a major literary epic, *Meghnād-badh kābya* ('The Poem of the Killing of Meghnād') by Michael Madhusudan Datta (1824-73), based on the *Rāmāyaṇa* but deeply influenced by Homer, Virgil, Dante and Milton. Tagore had cut his teeth as a literary critic with two harsh critiques of Madhusudan's epic, published in the journal *Bhāratī* in 1877 and 1882. He was perhaps never fully reconciled to it, but he came to accept its canonical status and knew that it would be hard to equal. A third answer could have been that the tedious, nationalistic epic poetry of Nabinchandra Sen (1847-1909) had given the genre a bad name. But in a poem in *Kṣaṇikā* (1900) entitled *Kṣati-pūraṇ*

1

('Compensation'), Tagore wittily lays the blame on his essentially lyrical muse:

> I had been toying
> With the thought of writing
>   An epic —
>
>   Until,
>   Stumbling at the jingle
>   Of your anklets and bangles,
>   My musings were shattered
>   Into songs innumerable:
>   Through that mishap
>   My epic was scattered
>   As particles
>   Round your feet.
>
>   I had been toying
>   With the thought of writing
>   An epic....

Underlying these lines is the comprehensiveness of Tagore's poetic ambition, his desire to achieve creative *purṇatā* or 'fullness' on an almost cosmic scale; but at the same time a tendency for that fullness to be expressed not in a single great work but in an endless stream of smaller ones. The epic vision that he undoubtedly possessed has been broken by his muse into separate grains or particles that together make up the whole, and which each perhaps contains the potential for the whole.

The word used for 'particle' in this poem is *kaṇā*; its diminutive — implying even smaller particles — is *kaṇikā*, which Tagore used as the title of the first of three books of poems in which, more than in any other book that he wrote, the large is expressed through the small. The present volume is a translation of all three. What English word best describes these poems? Some people have called them epigrams; but the gnomic, ironic, often malicious connotations of the epigram, aptly conveyed by Coleridge's definition, 'a dwarfish whole/Its body brevity, and wit its soul'[1] — are not, for the most part, appropriate for Tagore. 'Aphorism' is better, and may be valid for Tagore's own English translations of his poems of this sort, but the term is not usually applied to poetry, and every poem in the present volume is most definitely a poem, not a prose maxim or *pensée*. Moreover, the worldly yet subversive motive behind many aphorisms, particularly in the French tradition, is again not present in Tagore.[2]

Tagore himself coined the term *kabitikā* ('poemlet'), a diminutive of *kabitā* ('poem'). But that sounds too twee in English. We need a term that does not draw attention to itself unduly, but which is novel enough to capture the originality of Tagore's achievement in this genre, its uniqueness in world literature. I have decided to speak of his 'brief poems'. 'Brief' is more absolute

---

1. In an 'Original Epigram' first published in the *Morning Post*, 23 September 1802; quoted by Arun Kumar Basu in his study of Tagore's brief poems, *Kṣaṇiker bāṇī-śilpī Rabīndranāth* (Calcutta: Tagore Research Institute, 1987); included in *The Faber Book of Epigrams and Epitaphs*, edited by Geoffrey Grigson (London, 1977).
2. See John Gross's appropriately succinct introduction to his *Oxford Book of Aphorisms* (1983).

than 'short', which is too variable and relative a term to be useful here, unless we say 'very short poems'. 'Brief' also, through its rich literary associations, places the poems *sub specie aeternitatis*: the right context for them. Dictionary citations for 'brief' convey its flavour: 'Out, out, *breefe* Candle' (*Macbeth*); in the *Oxford English Dictionary*; 'How *brief* the life of man' (*Hamlet*); in *Webster's New International Dictionary*. Beyond English usage lies *Vita brevis ars longa* and other classical tags. Webster also gives a quotation from Ben Jonson that perfectly captures the character of Tagore's brief poems: 'The *brief* style is that which expresseth much in little.'

The stream that started with *Kaṇikā* continued to flow, amidst numerous other kinds of writing and activity, for the remaining forty-two years of Tagore's life. If we include *all* the brief poems that he wrote in many countries for friends, hosts, autograph-hunters, brides and bridegrooms, for children at their name-giving ceremonies, or as obituaries, we do not know exactly how many he wrote, as they are still being discovered and collected. But there are good reasons, as I shall argue later, for confining the category to the three books *Kaṇikā* ('Particles', 1899), *Lekhan* ('Jottings', 1927) and the first edition of *Sphuliṅga* ('Sparks', posthumously published in 1945).

Kaṇikā ('Particles') was published on the fourth day of the month of Agrahāyaṇ, 1306 B.E. (19 November 1899).[3] For the previous decade, Tagore had been living in the Padma river region of East Bengal, managing the family estates at Shelidah, Potisar and Sajadpur. By 1898 he had brought his wife and children to

---

3.   The Bengali Era begins in 593A.D., and the year starts in mid-April with the month of Baiśākh.

4

live in the house that the family owned at Shelidah.[4] Although Tagore had come to love the people, land and rivers of the region, and was inspired by them to write his finest short stories and letters, the end of the decade was a very difficult time for him. The combination of zamindari responsibilities, perilous business ventures, the demands of his young family, the death of his nephew Balendranath in August 1899 aged only twenty-nine, and the strain of conducting his literary career at such a distance from Calcutta, wore him out. He found it particularly difficult to shrug off the virulent criticisms of his writings that appeared in Calcutta's periodicals. In April 1898 he became editor of the journal *Bhāratī,* contributing many poems, short stories and essays; but a year later he resigned. His biographer Prabhat Kumar Mukhopadhay says that amidst such strain and difficulty the brief poems of *Kaṇikā* were all he could manage.[5]

In *Kaṇikā,* a book of 110 poems, the style and character of Tagore's later brief poems can be seen to evolve. But it would be wrong to see it merely as a kind of run-up to *Lekhan* and *Sphuliṅga.* Its transitional character makes it one of Tagore's most satisfying books — a subtle and balanced shape being given by the longer, lighter, fable-like poems at the beginning, the pithy and witty four-line and two-line poems in the middle, and the more serious, probing, cosmic poems at the end. Bengali critics have perhaps not taken it seriously enough. Sukumar Sen, in his authoritative history of Bengali literature (in the volume devoted to Tagore),

4. For more information on this period, see the Introduction to my *Selected Short Stories* of Tagore (Penguin, rev. ed. 1994).
5. *Rabīndrajībanī* (4th edition, 1970), vol.1, p.489.

says nothing about it at all.[6] I have come across only one detailed study of it.[7]

We do not know exactly when Tagore started to write the poems, but since one of them, 'The Stopping of Theft' (No. 15) was printed in the Kārtik issue of *Bhāratī,* 1305 (October-November 1898), it must have been at least a year before publication. Bengali critics find a lineage for the poems in Sanskrit and Prakrit literature: to a faint extent in the gnomic *ślokas* of Cāṇakya (though Tagore's poems are not nearly so didactic), but more strongly in *udbhaṭ* (anonymous, popular, traditional) *ślokas* of which two collections, the *Sadukti-karṇāmṛta* (in Sanskrit) and the *Gāthā-saptaśatī* (in Prakrit) were especially well known in Bengal.[8] Tagore's familiarity with Sanskrit wisecracks and apophthegms of this sort is evidenced by his early novel *Prajāpatir nirbandha* (serialised in *Bhāratī* in 1900-1901), which has a character called Rasik who spouts them.[9] Other classical influences were the Aesop-like animal fables of the famous Sanskrit collections *Pañcatantra* and *Hitopadeśa.* Tagore may also have encountered the fables of La Fontaine, either

6. Sukumar Sen, *Bāngālā sāhityer itihās*, vol.3 (Calcutta, 1946). There are just two passing references to *Kaṇikā* on p.117 and p.499.

7. Arun Kumar Basu, *op.cit.*, a perceptive study of all three books of brief poems, together with Tagore's late book of nonsense verse, *Khāpchāṛā* (1937).

8. Sanskrit is India's classical literary language. The various Prakrits, precursors of the modern South Asian languages, were colloquial relatives of Sanskrit, though some (such as the Buddhist language Pali) themselves became vehicles for literature.

9. In its serial form, the novel — much of which is written as dramatic dialogue — was called *Cirakumārasabhā.* Some twenty-five years later, Tagore turned it into a play with the same name.

through his brother Jyotirindranath Tagore (who knew French) or through the Bengali versions of some of them done by Michael Madhusudan Datta in the 1860s.

Kaṇikā seems to have temporarily disarmed critics of Tagore who said that his poetry lacked substance.[10] However, there is heavy irony in the response of Sureshchandra Samajpati, Tagore's most unrelenting critic, to a positive review of the book by Akshaykumar Maitra that had been published in the journal *Pradīp*.[11] Akshaykumar had expressed special sympathy for the sensitivity to malicious critics that is clearly discernible in a number of poems in *Kaṇikā*. Sureshchandra's rejoinder vividly brings out the literary warfare of the times:

> Akshay Babu has tried to demonstrate to the public that the poet wrote many of the poems in *Kaṇikā* to get his own back on his critics. If indeed Rabindra Babu were to produce writings of the order of *Kaṇikā* out of irritation with criticism, then the critics would have no cause for distress. We too have been obliged to say lots of good and bad things about Rabindra Babu's compositions. If because of the barbs of adverse criticism the immortal poet Rabindranath's divine stream of poetry makes Bengali literature verdant and fertile, then what greater joy for the critics can there be? But the truth-loving

---

10. Prasanta Kumar Paul, Tagore's leading biographer today, writes in his *Rabijībanī,* vol.4 (Calcutta, 1988), p.255: 'Those who had criticised the lack of substance in Tagore's writing were certainly pleasantly surprised when they received this volume...'

11. Māgh 1306 (January-February 1900), pp.61-63. See Prasanta Kumar Paul, *Rabijībanī,* vol.4 (Calcutta, 1988), p.242.

historian Akshay Babu will be sorry to hear that Rabindra Babu himself, having read Akshay Babu's critique, has said to us that he had no hidden motive of this sort. To allow Akshay Babu's assertion of a hidden aim in *Kaṇikā* to be placed on Rabindra Babu's shoulders without objection is to give refuge to insolence and baseness in literature: this is why we raise the matter. The notion that *Kaṇikā*'s jasmine and *mallikā*-clusters should bloom in the hell of pettiness, should spread their fragrance on the wind of malicious pique, that the writer should be capable of brazenly presenting this to the public in order to indulge his own aversion to critics, that he himself should engage in criticism, is surprising.[12]

In 1903 a collected edition of Tagore's poems to date was published in nine parts by S.C. Majumdar, edited by Mohitchandra Sen. The poems were arranged thematically, and Tagore prefaced twenty-six of the twenty-eight sections with a new poem.[13] The poem for *Kaṇikā* was as follows:

> 'Alas, O sun, who but the sky can embrace you?
> I see you in my dreams, but I cannot serve you.'
> > Thus said the dewdrop, weeping:
> > 'To hold you in my safe-keeping,
> > I don't have the strength, O sun.
> My tiny life is naught but a tear-drop without you.'

---

12. *Sāhitya*, Phālgun 1306 (February-March 1900), p.717; quoted by Prasanta Kumar Paul, *ibid.*, p.242.
13. These prefatory poems were later published in a separate collection, *Utsarga* ('Dedications', 1914).

'I light the whole of the earth with my huge rays,
Yet can let myself be embraced by a drop of dew:
        I *can* give my love to you.'
        Thus said the sun, smiling,
        The dew's heart entering:
        'By becoming so small, I'll fill you:
I'll make your tear-drop laughter, with my blaze.'

The poem expresses the 'big in small' content of the poems in *Kaṇikā*, but its mood and imagery (and the punning on his own name, *Rabi*, 'sun') belong more to the brief poems that Tagore was to start writing ten years later, foreshadowed by the lyrical, probing, cosmic poems that conclude the book.

Tagore's second book of brief poems (unless one counts his English collection, *Stray Birds*, 1916, of which more below), *Lekhan* had a much more complicated publishing history than *Kaṇikā*. In 1926, by then a Nobel Prize-winner and at the height of his international fame, Tagore made his eighth foreign tour from May to December, accompanied by his son Rathindranath and daughter-in-law Pratima Devi, the statistician Prasanta Chandra Mahalanobis with his wife Nirmalkumari ('Rani Devi') and others. He visited Naples, Rome, Florence, Turin, Villeneuve in Switzerland, Vienna, Dartington Hall in England, Oxford, Oslo, Stockholm, Copenhagen, Berlin, Munich, Nuremberg, Stuttgart, Cologne, Düsseldorf, Dresden, Prague and Budapest — where, not surprisingly, he fell ill from fatigue. On Sunday, 31 October, he retired to a sanatorium at Balatonfüred, Hungary. On 10 November he was well enough to return to Budapest, where he met the Governor of Hungary, Miklos Horthy, and on 11 November he left the country, travelling on to Zagreb, Belgrade, Sofia,

Bucharest, Constanza, Constantinople, Athens, Alexandria and Cairo. He sailed from Alexandria to Calcutta, and finally returned to his home at Santiniketan on Christmas Day.

While resting by Lake Balaton, he diverted himself by writing the Bengali and English poems of *Lekhan* directly on to aluminium sheets, using a stylus: a new printing technology that had been noticed by Prasanta Chandra Mahalanobis in Berlin. The sheets were then dispatched to Berlin, and separate facsimile pages were printed there but not bound. The following year, in Bengal, some copies were bound in leather and privately distributed (the surviving copies contain no mention of a publisher), but some pages were left out and others were in the wrong order. In Tagore's centenary year, 1961, blocks were made from the pages, and a new facsimile edition was published by Visva-Bharati, printed by the School of Printing Technology, Calcutta. The book was also incorporated into the centenary edition of Tagore's complete works, though not with the English versions.

The poems in *Lekhan* had been accumulating for over ten years. Sixteen had been written as early as 1912, for they were published in the journal *Prabāsī* under the title *Dvipadī* ('two-liners').[14] But Tagore started to write the rest during his fourth foreign tour, May 1916 to March 1917, to Burma, Japan, America (via the Pacific), and back to Japan. In his preface to the book, he associates them particularly with Japan and also with China

---

14. Agrahāyaṇ 1320. Twenty were printed there; seventeen of them became, in a different order, *Lekhan* Nos. 172 to 188 (with a couple of minor changes to Nos.179 and 188); another was the basis of No.189; the remaining two eventually became *Sphuliṅga* 58 and 182.

(which he visited in 1924). The English version of the preface reads: 'The lines in the following pages had their origin in China and Japan where the author was asked for his writings on fans and pieces of silk. Nov. 7, 1926, Balatonfüred, Hungary.' The longer Bengali version is as follows:

> These writings began in China and Japan. Their origin was in requests to write something on fans or pieces of paper or handkerchiefs. Thereafter I received demands in my own country and in other countries. In this way these piecemeal writings accumulated. Their chief value is to introduce myself through my own handwriting. But not only through my handwriting: through my swiftly written feelings too. In printed form this kind of personal contact is spoilt — these writings would seem as pallid and futile as an extinguished Chinese lantern. So when news came that in Germany there was a way of printing handwriting, the verses in *Lekhan* were reproduced. They contain some spontaneous corrections and crossings-out. Even these convey the flavour of my personality.[15]

Appendix A of the present volume (p.161) contains some other materials relating to the genesis of *Lekhan*: an essay by Tagore himself on the book, first published in *Prabāsī*, Kārtik 1335;[16] an extract from his travel diary, *Jāpān-yātrī* ('Traveller to

---

15. *Rabīndra-racanābalī* (Tagore's Collected Works), vol.14, p.156.
16. October-November 1928. The essay was reprinted by Visva-Bharati in the Notes at the end of vol.14 of *Rabīndra-racanābalī*.

Japan', 1919); and an extract from Nirmalkumari Mahalanobis's memoir of her travels with Tagore, *Kabir saṅge yūrope* ('To Europe with the Poet', 1969). From these we learn how impressed Tagore was by the seriousness with which very short *haiku* poems were taken in Japan, and how hosts and friends would press him for keepsake verses.[17]

In his *Prabāsī* article, Tagore disarmingly recounts how four poems by the poetess Priyambada Devi were inadvertently included in the first facsimile (private) edition of *Lekhan*; the first two lines of a fifth poem were also by her. When Visva-Bharati reprinted *Lekhan* in 1961, these rogue poems were removed. By mistake, one of Tagore's own poems was removed too (No.160 — 'I thought I would count the stars...'), probably because it was on

---

17. In addition, Dr Imre Bangha, a Hungarian scholar of Hindi who has researched Tagore's visit to Hungary, has supplied me with newspaper accounts. No journalists were allowed to visit Tagore at Balatonfüred, so reports were based on hearsay. A reporter in the newspaper *Nemzeti újság*, 27 October, wrote: 'I see with amazement that Tagore does not write on paper as other mortal poets. No, he values his writings more: he draws oriental characters with a corroding liquid on silver plates....An aristocratic attitude: to incise his thoughts on to metal at the moment of their birth.' Tagore's party included Baroness Lisa Pott from Germany, but it was not she who took the plates back to Berlin, for she accompanied the poet all the way to Santiniketan. An article in the journal *Balatoni Szemle* in May 1943 implies that they were posted, not taken by any individual: 'He wrote the poems on silver plates continuously, without correcting a letter. The plates were sent for printing to his publisher in Berlin in boxes especially prepared for this purpose....'

the same page as the five rogue poems. It was restored in the *Rabīndra-racanābalī*.[18]

Lekhan is Tagore's only bilingual book. It contains 142 poems both in English and Bengali, forty-seven in Bengali only and eighty-eight in English only.[19] Tagore was already well experienced at writing English versions of his brief poems, or sometimes writing them directly in English, for in 1916 Macmillan in New York published *Stray Birds*, a collection of 326 English aphorisms. (The term 'aphorism' is appropriate here, as they were all in prose, not verse.) It was a handsome book, with a wistful colour frontispiece by Willy Pogány, and elegant decorative fleurons on the pages. While he was in America, Tagore had written to the Director of Macmillan in New York, George Brett: 'I am sending you under cover by Registered Post the manuscript of a collection of short sayings and maxims in poetical form, which everyone who has seen them feels should be published before Christmas while I am still in this country. The title of the volume would be "Stray Birds and Withered Leaves" and it should be published in an attractive form.'[20] Attractiveness of production and design had become an important

18. There is, however, still some textual confusion with regard to *Lekhan*. In the *Rabīndra-racanābalī*, Nos.71-77 are for some unexplained reason placed *after* Nos. 78-103, and No.132 is not given a number at all. I have followed the West Bengal Government edition (vol.2, 1982).

19. According to my reckoning! Sisir Kumar Das, in *The English Writings of Rabindranath Tagore*, vol. 1, *Poems* (New Delhi: Sahitya Akademi, 1994), p.624, comes up with different figures.

20. Prasanta Kumar Paul, vol. 7, p.197.

selling-point in Tagore's Western career. Macmillan's advertisement for its new 'Bolpur edition' of Tagore's works stated: 'Great care has been taken with the physical appearance of the books...Altogether this edition promises to become the standard one of this distinguished poet and seer.'[21] *Fireflies*, a similar book of 256 English aphorisms, published in 1928, was even more exquisite, with intricate (matching but varied) arabesques by Boris Artzybasheff on every page.[22]

Stray Birds was dedicated to T. Hara of Yokohama, Tagore's host in 1916-17. On 26 June 1916, W. W. Pearson, one of his companions on the trip, had written to Rathindranath from Yokohama: 'Gurudev [Tagore] has been in to us once or twice with some aphorisms which he has been writing on golden cards which have been given to him by our host for Gurudev to write something on.'[23] Many of the aphorisms it contains — as in *Fireflies* and the English parts of *Lekhan* — have no Bengali source, though the majority do. Many of the English versions in *Lekhan* (which was never published in the West) were re-used in *Fireflies* (sometimes slightly revised); the book's title was taken from *Lekhan*'s opening poem; and it was prefaced with a similar explanatory sentence.[24] Moreover, the posthumous collection *Sphuliṅga*, of which more below, includes Bengali versions of a

---

21. *Stray Birds* (New York; The Macmillan Company, 1916), endpapers.
22. The German editions published by Kurt Wolff Verlag were equally beautiful.
23. Prasanta Kumar Paul, vol.7, p.196.
24. 'Fireflies had their origin in China and Japan where thoughts were very often claimed from me in my handwriting on fans and pieces of silk.'

number of poems that had previously only appeared in English. So Sisir Kumar Das, in his new edition of Tagore's English writings, is justified in saying that the four books — *Stray Birds, Lekhan, Fireflies* and *Sphuliṅga* — 'form one significant unit'.[25] But what exactly *is* the status of the English versions vis-à-vis the Bengali? And do they have any relevance to the present volume, an attempt to translate all three books of Bengali brief poems afresh, into verse, not prose?

This is not the place to raise the whole controversial question of Tagore's own translations, though I believe his expressions of regret, late in life, that he had done them at all, should always be included in the debate.[26] But for anyone with a knowledge of Bengali as well as English, reading the aphorisms, no less than Tagore's other translations, is a frustrating business.

Given that he was a Bengali poet, not an English one, his method of translating his brief Bengali poems into prose, not verse, is fully understandable. The method evolved over time. The very earliest translations of them that he published, in the *Modern Review* in 1912 and 1913, were longer and more poem-like than his translations later became, though the editor of the journal, Ramananda Chatterjee, appears to have had a hand in

25. *Op. cit.*, p.616.

26. See, for example his letter to William Rothenstein on 26 November 1932, in *Imperfect Encounter: Letters of William Rothenstein and Rabindranath Tagore*, edited by Mary Lago (Harvard, 1972), p. 346; or his letters to Sturge Moore (14 May 1921) or Edward Thompson (5 August 1921) in *Selected Letters of Rabindranath Tagore*, edited by Krishna Dutta and Andrew Robinson (Cambridge, 1997), p. 272 and p.275.

them.[27] Take this one, for example, a translation of *Kaṇikā*
No.33 ('Egalitarianism'):

> Said the beggar's wallet, 'Come, my brother purse,
> Between us two the difference is so very small,
> Let us exchange!' The purse snapped short and sharp,
> 'First let that very small difference cease.'[28]

But Tagore abandoned this way of translating and instead strove
to reduce his Bengali brief poems to a simple English statement.
Some of the alterations to sayings in *Lekhan* re-used in *Fireflies*
are in the cause of greater simplification, and in all cases line-
endings are removed. For example, *Fireflies* No.187:

> Listen to the prayer of the forest for its freedom in flowers.

in *Lekhan* (No.129) was:

> I hear the prayer to the sun
> from the myriad buds in the forest:
>   'Open our eyes.'

---

27. They were all from *Kaṇikā*. The first group of eight (*Modern
    Review*, April 1912, p.351) were published anonymously, under the
    title 'Sparks from the Anvil'. The second group of twenty-five,
    published in November 1913 *post*-Nobel Prize, were proudly headed:
    'Poems by Rabindranath Tagore: Englished by the poet himself'.
    But Prasanta Kumar Paul (vol.6, p.276) quotes an undated letter
    from Tagore to Ramananda which thanks him for improving them:
    'By scrubbing and polishing them from start to finish you've almost
    created them afresh....'
28. From the second group, *Modern Review*, November 1913, pp.431-
    434.

This process was still going on at the end of his life. A copy of the first (1927) edition of *Lekhan*, in which Tagore wrote new Bengali versions of some of the English verses, also contains further revisions and simplifications to the English, suggesting that he was thinking about a new edition.[29]

Some of Tagore's English versions of his brief poems are beautiful and memorable in themselves, and it's probably best to think of them as an entirely different creative effort rather than a translation. But a few examples from *Stray Birds* of aphorisms based on poems in *Kaṇikā* indicate the problems if one starts to compare them with the original.

(No.71)
The woodcutter's axe begged for its handle from the tree.
　　　The tree gave it.

This is based on the six-line poem 'Politics' (*Kaṇikā* No.13). The axe's aggressive 'return of the favour' is omitted completely.

(No.129)
Asks the Possible to the Impossible, 'Where is your dwelling place?'
　　　'In the dreams of the impotent,' comes the answer.

Based on 'Unbearably Good' (No.43): the malicious envy of the detractors of 'Better-still' is lost.

---

29. Ms.388 in Rabindra Bhavana, Santiniketan. There is no date given to these changes, but a pen self-portrait opposite the first page is dated 7 Pauṣ 1345 (23 December 1938).

(No.163)
'The Learned say that your lights will one day be no more,'
said the firefly to the stars.
      The stars made no answer.

Based on the eight-line 'Incomplete Information' (No.9). The
cakorī-bird has been changed to firefly; moon to stars; their answer
is omitted; the humour is entirely lost.

(No.173)
'Who drives me forward like fate?'
      'The Myself striding on my back.'

Based on 'The Driver' (No.98); almost nonsensical.

(No.240)
Rockets, your insult to the stars follows yourself back to
earth.

Based on 'Arrogance' (No.45); wit and point lost.
    The translations in *Lekhan* are more accurate, but precisely
because the Bengali and English are side by side, the discrepancies
and unclarities are no less maddening. Why is No.15 so bafflingly
different from the original?

  White and pink oleanders meet
  and make merry in different dialects.

What does No.7 actually *mean*?

  My thoughts, like sparks,
      ride on winged surprises
         carrying a single laughter.

'Sparks' (*Sphulinga*) became the title of Tagore's last (posthumous) collection of brief poems, and the Bengali version of the last poem above was used as an epigraph. The collection's publishing history is almost as complicated as *Lekhan*'s, and it is to this that I now turn.

Sphulinga was first published on 25 Baiśākh 1352 (7 May 1945) — Tagore's birthday, four years after his death. It is a beautiful little book, 4.25 by 5.25 inches in size, with Boris Gorgieff's drawing of Tagore inside the front cover, endpapers by Nandalal Bose, and a delicate painting of a rose (by Tagore himself) as a frontispiece. It consists of 198 brief poems, arranged in alphabetical order of their initial letters. The note at the end begins as follows:

In 1334 *Lekhan* was published. Many more poems similar to *Lekhan* were for a long time scattered in various manuscripts of Rabindranath, in journals and in the collections of those dear to him or who had sought his blessing. Sri Kanai Samanta, Sri Pulinbihari Sen and Sri Prabhatchandra Gupta gathered many of these writings from various manuscripts and autograph-books and published them in periodicals; and those with poems of this sort in their own collections have also published them in journals. *Sphulinga* is a compendium of all these.

Before *Lekhan* was published, *Sphulinga* was considered as a title for the book.[30] This name has been adopted for the present volume. Its introductory poem has been taken from *Lekhan*.[31]

---

30. This is confirmed by Nirmalkumari Mahalanobis's Memoir. See Appendix A, p.172.
31. The poem quoted above (p.18, *Lekhan* No.7) that uses the word *Sphulinga*. It is reproduced in Tagore's own handwriting.

It is difficult to determine the date of composition of most of the poems; it cannot be said that they were actually composed on the dates that are given with the poems in the poet's own handwriting in his various manuscript collections. Many poems were written later than *Lekhan*, some were contemporary with it, some have been gathered from much older manuscripts...

The note goes on to give details of some of the sources of the poems: manuscripts of other books of poems, Tagore's book on metre, *Chanda* (1936), in which twenty-one of the poems first appeared as specimens of different metres; a painting in which Poem No.10 was inscribed; a French source (unnamed) for No.110. There follows a list of individuals who supplied poems from their own files. Nirmalkumari Mahalanobis and Satyajit Ray are thanked for the manuscripts of Nos. 4 and 127, reproduced in the book.

For the centenary edition of the *Rabīndra-racanābalī* (1961), Visva-Bharati expanded *Sphuliṅga* to 260 poems, and this became the 'standard' edition, whose numbering is used in other books such as Sisir Kumar Das's edition of Tagore's English works. Volume 3 of the West Bengal Government edition of Tagore's complete works (1983) contains the same text, and it was this that I first used, translating all of the 260 poems. In 1990 Visva-Bharati brought out a greatly expanded edition, with 410 poems. Volume 15 of the West Bengal Government edition (1994) has an appendix headed *Sphuliṅga 2* containing 299 poems. More are still being discovered and published.[32]

---

32. Notably by Gopalchandra Ray. His book *Rabīndranāther Sphuliṅga* (Calcutta, 1995) contains forty-six additions.

After considerable thought and after discussing the matter with Prasanta Kumar Paul and others, I have decided to stick to the first edition of 1945, with its 198 poems, for the following reasons.

It is difficult to know how much Tagore at the end of his life was involved in the selection of the poems, but he certainly gave his approval to the book in principle and to its title. The role of Pulinbihari Sen (1908-84) as one of its main compilers — a close associate of Tagore and a pioneering editor and bibliographer of his works — is assurance enough that the first edition accurately reflected Tagore's intention.

The problem with the second edition — and even more so with the third — is that many short poems have been added that do not really blend with the essential character of *Sphuliṅga*. Tagore wrote numerous short poems on all sorts of occasions, but that is not to say that they are all *Sphuliṅga* poems. Many of them are specific to a person or event; they might pun on a name or make a local reference; they might be light and humorous, or in the style of his book of nonsense verse *Khāpchāṛā* (1937). People kept them, but there are some such verses by Tagore which gently mocked autograph-hunters for preserving verses so ephemeral and trivial. For example:

> Why fill your bags with my every verbal scrap?
> Things that belong to the dust should be left to drop.[33]

Of course all lovers of Tagore are grateful that such poems have not been allowed to drop. In Appendix C, I give a particularly

33. The background to this and a number of other collected and uncollected verses by Tagore is given by Subrata Rudra in *Kṣaṇakāler chanda* (Calcutta, 1978).

charming example, hitherto unpublished in the version that was shown to me. It thanks a friend for a gift of *āmsattva* (crystalised mango-juice); it is affectionate, witty and musical, but it does not belong to *Sphuliṅga*.

To stick to the first edition, therefore, results in a collection that is much more consistent and coherent than any of the later expansions. Many of the poems (from the second edition) that I have jettisoned are fine in themselves, but the balance not only of *Sphuliṅga* but the whole of the present volume is, I think, better without them.

The true *Sphuliṅga* poems have a character, spirit, quality or — as Bengalis would put it — a *bhāba* that is general in implication, not specific. They may mostly have stemmed from occasions, but only those that transcend their occasion deserve a place in *Sphuliṅga*. On 8 November 1926, for example, while Tagore was at Balatonfüred, he planted a linden-tree by the lake, announcing: 'I am planting this tree in remembrance of my stay here, for nowhere else was I given what I received here. It was more than hospitality, it was awakening of feelings of kinship. I sense and I know that I have come to the land of a nation which is emotionally akin to India...' On returning to his hotel he wrote in the visitors' book what was to become Poem No.196 in *Sphuliṅga*, one of its loveliest, with an English prose rendering: 'When I am no longer on the earth, my tree, let the ever-renewed leaves of thy spring murmur to the wayfarers: "The poet did love while he lived."'[34] The tree still flourishes, and is a place of pilgrimage for visiting

---

34. Prabhat Kumar Mukhopadhay, *Rabīndrajībanī*, vol.3 (3rd ed., Calcutta, 1990), p.289.

Indians and all admirers of Tagore; the poem is given additional beauty by its context, but is not dependent on it.

What, then, is the *bhāba* of *Sphuliṅga*? Through Tagore's three books of Bengali brief poems we watch it steadily taking shape, and the first thing to say about it is that it required, for its full expression, extraordinary metrical and formal flexibility. The poems in *Kaṇikā* were all written in the traditional Bengali *payār* metre: fourteen syllables per line, seven feet, the lines rhymed in couplets. *Lekhan* used three basic metres, but with increasing variety in rhyme and line-length.[35] In *Sphuliṅga* virtually every one of the 198 poems is different in form. That alone is a breathtaking achievement.

Their concise lucidity is also a most striking feature. Tagore's poetry can be highly elaborate, but in these brief poems he expressed his essential ideas and feelings in the simplest possible way. In reading his longer poems, or his essays and lectures in Bengali and English, one often comes across passages that echo, in more words, one or other of his brief poems. Often an idea is conveyed by the form as well as the words. For example, Paragraph 160 in *Thoughts from Tagore*,[36] in which he writes, 'Life, which is

---

35. 'The poet has used three kinds of metre; moreover, in each composition — in its stanzaic inventiveness, rhyme scheme and arrangement of lines — technical skill is readily apparent. The poems are normally between two and twelve lines in length.' Arun Kumar Basu, *op. cit.*, p.34.

36. A book of prose reflections, some of them based on Bengali essays, first published by Macmillan, New York in 1921 under the title *Thought Relic*. It was expanded and republished in 1929 as *Thoughts from Tagore*. See Sisir Kumar Das, *op. cit.*, vol.3, *A Miscellany* (1996).

an incessant explosion of freedom, finds its metre in continual falling back in death...', is expressed rhythmically in *Kaṇikā* 94: 'Birth and death, taking turns, make life's game...'. Poems about birthdays (e.g. Nos. 62 and 96 in *Sphuliṅga*) express by their formal completeness as well as by their words Paragraph 89 in the same book:

> A young friend of mine comes to me this morning to inform me that it is his birthday and that he has just reached his nineteenth year. The distance between my age and his is great, and yet when I look at him it is not the incompleteness of his life which strikes me, but something which is complete in his youth. And in this differs the thing which grows, from the thing which is being made. A building in its unfinished stage is only too evidently unfinished. But in life's growth every stage has its perfection, the flower as well as the fruit.

To go, however, more deeply into the *bhāba* of the brief poems, it is helpful to consider the full meaning of this word. It was already rich in meanings and associations in Sanskrit, and in Bengali it has acquired still more. The Samsad Bengali-English dictionary[37] gives the following: 'birth, origination; existence, presence, essence, shape; intention, state, condition; mental state, mood; nature; love, attachment, friendship, amity; acquaintance; manner, mode; inner significance, implication, an idea; an abstract idea or thought, imagination; meditation, cogitation; reverie, ecstasy; emotion, an outburst of emotion; (amongst children) amity, peace.' From this it can be seen firstly that *bhāba* includes

---

37. Calcutta, 1968.

24

both thought and feeling, idea and emotion; secondly that it is used both for *varieties* of thought or feeling and for a *general* quality. In this it is like 'poetry' or 'music', which can be used for different varieties (sad music, happy music, epic poetry, lyric poetry) but also for something general. When we talk of 'the music of the spheres' or of architecture as 'frozen music', or when Coleridge's Ancient Mariner says: 'No voice; but oh! the silence sank/Like music on my heart', something *general* is meant, and we know what it is.

It seems to me that in Tagore's brief poems we have this *general* quality of *bhāba*, as well as, of course, a variety of different ideas, moods and feelings. They therefore take us right to the centre of his poetry. Often when he felt burdened by all the responsibilities and activities he took on to himself, he would protest that he was 'just a poet'. To his friend C. F. Andrews, for example, he wrote from Chicago on 24 February, 1921: 'Why should I be anything else but a poet? Was I not born a music-maker?'[38] Unfortunately, as Sisir Kumar Das rightly says, 'the truth was he was not only a poet.'[39] In his brief poems, however, he *was* only a poet, and this is why his voice in them is so free, so natural, so spontaneous and so friendly.

The meaning of 'friendship' that *bhāba* has (especially in Bengali) is relevant here. Many of the poems were acts of friendship, so friendship is in their essential nature. Through them, Tagore extends the hand of friendship to his readers, reveals himself in a particularly direct and natural way. This is what he

---

38. C. F. Andrews (ed.), *Letters to a Friend* (New York, 1929), p.125.
39. *Op. cit.,* vol.3, Introduction, p.17.

meant in his Bengali preface to *Lekhan*, speaking of 'introducing' himself through them. And the word in that passage that I translated as 'feelings' is *bhāba*.[40]

The friendliness of Tagore's brief poems can, I believe, be conveyed in translation, but only if it is done as a reciprocal act of friendship. If the translator is grudging, thoughtless or impatient, he will not be able to capture their sparkling yet tender spirit.

What is their place in world literature? How do they relate to the mass of poetry that we regard as native to the twentieth century? What relevance do they have to the twenty-first century?

When Tagore won the Nobel Prize with *Gitanjali* in 1913, and quickly reached an immense worldwide readership through his English translations (which were in turn translated into other languages), those who were drawn to him found in him a kind of one-man counter-culture: an alternative to their own societies and the modernist literature that they were producing. This perception was not entirely wrong; Tagore was, and still is, a counter-culture. What was not well understood was that (a) he was a counter-culture within his own society just as much, if not more so, than he was in the West, and (b) his art and ideas were by no means an *inevitable* product of India's cultural and literary traditions. His promoters and admirers saw the poetry of *Gitanjali* as the natural, inevitable product of a tradition and a society radically different from the West. W. B. Yeats, in his famous Introduction to *Gitanjali*, wrote:

> These lyrics — which are in the original, my Indians tell me, full of subtlety of rhythm, of untranslatable delicacies of colour, of metrical invention — display in their thought a

---

40. See above, p.11.

world I have dreamed of all my life long. The work of a supreme culture, they yet appear as much the growth of the common soil as the grass and the rushes.[41]

O. E. Lessing, in the first German article on Tagore, written after the publication of *Gitanjali* but before the Nobel Prize, used similar language, even though he recognised Tagore's progressive modernity in the sphere of education:

> One feels in it the heritage of an ancient culture, which seeks to value all appearances of life according to their inner worth. His transcendentalism and mysticism have nothing of the illness of overheated ecstasy and suicidal asceticism of Christian-romantic Europeans....
>
> Tagore is perhaps the last great poet of ancient India....[42]

Yeats, Lessing and many other Westerners remained ignorant of the complex hybrid culture of nineteenth-century Bengal from which Tagore emerged, and they did not appreciate that the elements in India's traditions — the Upanishads, Kalidasa, medieval Bengali Vaishnavism, the songs of the wandering Bauls — that he

---

41. *Gitanjali* (London: The India Society, 1912; Macmillan, 1913), Introduction.
42. My translation. This essay, 'Rabindra Nath Tagore', published on 1 June, 1913 in the journal *Das literarische Echo*, was written from Urbana, Illinois, where Lessing had met Tagore in the winter of 1912-13. It has been rediscovered by Martin Kämpchen, who quotes it in connection with Tagore's German publisher Kurt Wolff in *Rabindranath Tagore in Germany: four responses to a cultural icon* (Shimla: Indian Institute of Advanced Study, 1999), p.66. I am grateful to him for giving me a copy of the article.

emphasised were *chosen* by him, or had been chosen before him by his father Debendranath and other leading figures of the Bengal Renaissance. There were many other elements that he could have chosen, and some of them were conspicuous by their absence: the *Bhagavad-gītā*, for example, very popular with late nineteenth-century Hindu revivalists; or the worship of the goddesses Kali or Durga; or Hindu Bengal's major religious festival, *Durgā-pūjā*.[43] His works were conscious, deliberate and sophisticated, not the innocent products of a pre-modern society.

He was, indeed, far more modern than he appeared. Take, for example, his deep interest in science. This is a huge subject in itself, and I have written about it elsewhere.[44] In his English lectures, Tagore often spoke of the limitations of science, and this — together with his dislike of an industrialised 'machine-culture' — may sometimes have given the impression that he was sceptical about it or even hostile to it. But in fact he was fascinated by science throughout his life and was very knowledgeable about

43. Kali appears in his play *Bisarjan* ('Sacrifice', 1890), but in an extremely negative light. There are references to *Durgā-pūjā* in his short stories (see, for example, 'Fool's Gold' in my *Selected Short Stories* of Tagore), and an eloquent letter to Indira Devi about the festival (5 October 1894; *Chinnapatrābalī*, Visva-Bharati, new ed. 1993, pp.241-2). But in the letter, positive though it is, Tagore writes as an outsider: his Brahmo background excluded him. By and large, Bengali Shaktism (worship of the mother-goddess) is absent from Tagore. Like the *Bhagavad-gītā*, it had been tainted for him, perhaps, by Hindu revivalism.

44. See my lecture, 'Particles and Sparks: Tagore, Einstein and the poetry of science', in *India International Centre Quarterly*, vol.25 nos.2 & 3 (Summer-Monsoon 1998), pp.131-150.

it. Much of his early journalism was on scientific subjects; his friendship with the physicist and plant physiologist Jagadish Chandra Bose was one of his closest; he was keen that modern scientific know-how should be applied to his rural development projects; his personal library included many books on science and even on mathematics;[45] and at the end of his life he wrote a lucid account of modern science, *Biśva-paricay* ('Discovering the Universe', 1937), which was remarkably up-to-date, particularly on the structure of the atom. Scientific themes and allusions abound in his poetry,[46] and the brief poems in this book frequently touch on cosmic and natural phenomena in a way that has an obvious scientific context, once one becomes attuned to it.[47]

Science interested Tagore not just because he was fascinated by the cosmos and its processes, but because the scientific stance of detachment matched his own poetic ideal. In the poems in the present book there is much that is sensitive and personal, but that is because the poet's own experiences and feelings are as much a subject for observation and reflection as are Nature and the

45. Annotations in the books show that he read them carefully. Tagore's personal library is preserved at Rabindra Bhavana, Santiniketan, and has been listed in *Rabindra-Bhavana Collection Catalogue-in-Progress,* vols. 1-3 (1982, 1982, 1983).

46. In my *Selected Poems* of Tagore (Penguin, 1985), see especially 'Brāhma, Viṣṇu, Śiva', 'In Praise of Trees', 'Earth' and '*The Sick-bed — 21*', with my notes on these poems.

47. The title *Kaṇikā* did not at the time the book was published (1899) imply subatomic particles, but in view of Tagore's interest in science, the acquisition of this association later does not seem to me inappropriate.

Universe. Any complete account of the universe must, Tagore insisted, include human *bodha* or consciousness. But he was interested only in personal feelings that were of *general* significance — part of the commonly shared *bhāba* that makes us human. Just as science discounts individual fantasies in its pursuit of truth, so poetry, in its purest form, must be detached, general, free of personal idiosyncrasy; must express what Tagore called 'the Universal Man'.[48]

We see this spirit of detachment emerging and strengthening in the course of his three books of brief poems. No one should suppose (as his contemporary Western admirers often did) that Tagore was personally free of tension and conflict, anxiety and insecurity.[49] Some of those tensions and sensitivities are readily apparent in the conflicts and oppositions in *Kaṇikā*, and they are not entirely absent from *Sphuliṅga*. If we remember that 'Rabi' means the sun, we can detect from No.118, for example, how sensitive Tagore remained till the end of his days to misunderstanding and mockery. But the overall *bhāba* of *Sphuliṅga* leaves such tensions behind.

The confused, dark side of life — with its tensions and conflicts — has dominated twentieth-century art and literature. Tagore was

---

48. Tagore used this phrase in his conversations in 1930 with Albert Einstein.

49. Bengali critics and biographers have been shy of probing Tagore's psychology. An exception is Manasi Dasgupta's book *Rabīndranāth: ek asamamvita dvandva* ('Rabindranath: an unresolved conflict', Dhaka: Sahityasamabay, 1987), which sees Tagore's unrelenting efforts in the practical sphere as stemming partly from fear of his father's disapproval of purely literary activity.

well aware of this. His late essay on modern poetry, which I have translated in Appendix B (p.173), shows how clear his understanding of literary modernism was. He knew what it was, admired some of its products, but chose to go in a different direction: not back to the Romantics of the nineteenth century, but forward to a new reconciliation of religion and rationalism, poetry and science — to the *pūrṇatā* ('fullness') that at the beginning of this Introduction I said was the goal of all his endeavours.

Which way do we now want poetry and literature to go? On with the collapsed romantic confusion and chaos of the twentieth century? Or forward to a new kind of classicism, a sense of order and unity supported by science and the ever-increasing interconnectedness and 'globalisation' of our world? On with forms of artistic expression radically divorced from Nature, or brought into harmony with our growing sense that we are responsible for the health and future of the natural world — a sense that has been enriched by science, but has also been stimulated by shame at science's misuse? I think there can be no doubt which way Tagore wanted to go, and it was forward, not back, employing — as he says at the end of his essay on modern poetry — the 'detached mind' that he saw in science but not yet in modern literature.

Detached, but not cold, not empty of sensitivity, warmth and feeling; and not empty of moral values either. Therein the *difference* between poetry and science, the reason why, in Tagore's view, science needs poetry, just as much as poetry needs science.

In Germany, just before and during the Second World War, when the Tagore *Rummel* (hullabaloo) had faded and his works were banned by the Nazis, a now scarcely remembered husband and wife team laboured to understand and present Tagore properly.

31

Helene Meyer-Franck translated his poems and prose, learning Bengali so as to be able to do this from the original; her husband, Heinrich Meyer-Benfey, a distinguished professor of literature with a knowledge of Sanskrit, wrote interpretative essays. They corresponded with Tagore, and met him twice. Their books are mostly forgotten. Only Martin Kämpchen, through his painstaking research on all aspects of Tagore's relationship with Germany, has noticed and appreciated their work.[50] Helene Meyer-Franck's last book of translations of Tagore, a slim selection of poems exquisitely translated into German lyric verse, came out in 1946. At the end of her brief foreword, penned in Buxtehude amidst the ruins of defeated Germany, she wrote:

> He knows that Dying does not lead to Death, but that Death can signify Life. He knows that in every person's soul — even in the worst criminal's soul — from somewhere within it, from a small hidden corner, the voice of Goodness, the voice of God calls; and what is more, that in everyone, even in the most unregenerate ṣoul, it is as the voice of Goodness that this voice is perceived. This gives him the assurance that Goodness is the principle of the World. And people need no more than that, in order to find peace and harmony of soul.[51]

Perhaps amidst the many other qualities of Tagore's brief poems — as in the poems that Helene Meyer-Franck translated — a

---

50. In ch.3 of *Rabindranath Tagore in Germany*. See fn.42 above.
51. My translation. From Rabindranath Tagore, *Mit meinen Liedern hab ich dich gesucht: Gedichte*, aus dem Bengalischen übertragen von Helene Meyer-Franck (Hamburg: Deutscher Literatur-Verlag, 1946), p.8.

quality of *goodness* is what shines forth most strongly. It sets him apart from most other twentieth-century poets; it may be what in years to come readers will most value in him.

That and a sense of mystery. In a Bengali essay on 'the changing state of poetry', written as early as 1881, Tagore wrote of how with each advance in science the mystery of the universe we inhabit advances too. That was one reason why science intrigued him so much, why he felt that poetry — far from being defeated — can thrive in an age of scientific advance. The further the light of knowledge advances, the closer it brings us to the darkness that in Poem No.109 in *Kaṇikā* is even more primary than light, and which may indeed be poetry's ultimate source. In his own words:

> What does the light of science do? It just 'makes the darkness visible': science is continually discovering darkness. The map of darkness is constantly growing: the great Columbuses of science are revealing new continents of darkness. For the night-bird of poetry, what happier time can there be! It loves mystery, and what greater mysteries ever existed in times past! In the uncovering of one mystery, ten more mysteries emerge.[52]

My experience of living with Tagore's brief poems and translating them over the last three years has been similar. The more pellucid and meaningful they have become, the greater their mystery.

W. R.

---

52. Quoted by Parimal Goswami in *Rabīndranāth o bijñān* (Calcutta, 1970), p.21. The essay was included in *Samālocanā* (1888).

Particles

(Kaṇikā, 1899)

1 **True Relationship**
The pumpkin supposes his bamboo-frame
Is a flying flower-chariot; proudly disdains
To look at the ground; thinks himself friendly
With moon, sun and stars. Believing he's really
Related to them, he stares at the sky
And wistfully thinks: 'It's just that I'm tied
To the earth by this great fat leaf-stalk — else
I'd fly to my own starry world in a trice.'
But when the stalk's cut, the truth sinks in:
Earth is his relative, not the sun.

2 **The Limits of Power**
The bell-metal water-pot chimes a question:
'Why, Uncle Well, are you not an ocean?
I could then plunge into you unhesitatingly,
Drink my fill of you, freely and greedily.'
'True', says the well, 'I'm not very grand:
That's why I don't talk. But why, young friend,
Should my smallness affect you? Keep coming down!
Take what you want, again and again!
However often you drink your fill,
I'll have enough water here for you still.'

3 **New Lifestyle**
The buffalo roars at the top of his voice,
'Why can't I have a groom like a horse?
This bovine existence is driving me mad —
Give me a twice-daily massage instead!'
He frets like this at the start of each day,
Stomping and champing to get his way.
His master says in the end, 'Very well —'
Sets ten men to groom him from head to tail.
Two days of this, and he wails, 'Master,
There's no need for more, I get the picture,
For God's sake tell the grooms to lay off!
The massage they've given is more than enough.'

4 **The Risks of Idleness**
The plough-handle yells at the blade in a temper,
'Where oh where have you come from, brother?
Ever since you and I were joined
I've had to keep sticking my head in the ground.'
'Very well,' says the blade, 'I'll cut myself loose.
Let's see what you'll gain from idleness!'
The blade breaks off; the handle is pleased
To settle down to a life of ease.
The farmer says, 'What's this rubbish here?
I'll use it today to light the fire.'
'O Blade,' says the handle, 'come back quick.
I'd rather be a slave than a kindling-stick!'

5 **Defeat and Victory**

The bee and the hornet broke out in dispute.
Whose power was the greater? 'A thousand proofs,'
The hornet sneered, 'show that your sting
Compared to mine is not at all strong.'
The bee had no answer. Seeing his tears
The Goddess of the Forest whispered in his ear:
'Why, my sweet, are you so cast down?
In poison you lose, but in honey you win.'

6 **Glory's Burden**

The tailorbird said, 'O Peacock, I feel
Such pity for you when I see your tail.'
Said the peacock, 'Really? Please tell me why
Seeing me brings a tear to your eye.'
The tailorbird said, 'It looks so funny —
Your tail much greater in size than your body.
Just watch how *I* dart lightly about!
Your tail must be such a burdensome weight.'
'Don't,' said the peacock, 'grieve for me falsely.
Burdens must rest on those who have glory.'

7 **Worm's Judgement**

A bookworm has entered the *Mahābhārat,*
Chewed and holed it inside and out.
The *paṇḍit,* opening it, beats his brow:
'What, O worm, are you playing at now?
To sharpen your teeth and fill your belly
The earth already supplies you fully!'

The worm replies, 'Why get so cross?
Are little black dots so great a loss?
Whatever I can't understand is rubbish:
I gnaw and chew it until I finish.'[1]

8 **Proper Duty**
'Honestly, sir,' says Umbrella to Head,
'The unfairness of it is really too bad.
You swan around happily, safe and free,
While rain and sun pour down on me.
Were *you* an umbrella, what would you think?'
'I'd respect,' says Head, 'the importance of rank.
A headless world could never function.
I'd find in *your* role a great distinction!'

9 **Incomplete Information**
The *cakorī*[2] weeps, 'Divine full moon,
What the *paṇḍits* say afflicts me with pain.
To think one day you'll be gone from heaven,
That your light will end at the Great Destruction.
O fount of nectar, Lord of night,
How miserable then will be our plight!'
Moon says, 'My dear, go back to the *paṇḍit* —
Ask him about your *own* life's limit.'

---

1. The *Mahābhārata* is the Great Epic of India, the longest and most
    influential classical Indian epic. A *paṇḍit* is a scholar, traditionally
    a teacher of Sanskrit.
2. A kind of bird that is said to enjoy drinking moonlight.

10 Jealousy's Suspicions

It maddens a dog to see in a mirror
A rival who's just as good a tail-wagger.
Whenever a servant flicks flies with a whisk,
He thinks in his fury, 'What wretch is this?'
At the swishing of trees or rippling of water,
He barks and barks with jealous anger.
He's certain the whole world's eager as he
To jump up on to his master's knee —
But damnit, those leavings are *his* to gobble!
Only *his* tail has the right to waggle!

11 The Greatest Claim

A debate between plants has gone on all day:
In the forest who has the greatest sway?
Says the *bakul,* 'Friends, it's clear to all,
The forest lies under my perfume's rule.'
Says the scentless *palās,* 'I disagree.
My colour commands — look round and see!'
Blushing with fury, the rose joins in:
'With my colour *and* scent, *I* surely win!'
'Scent? Beauty? That's all bosh!'
The *kacu* retorts. 'My roots push
My claim all over the forest's floor.
Look at the proof!' They argue no more.[3]

---

3. *Bakul*-trees produce small, white, sweetly scented flowers; *palās*-flowers are beautiful and red but have no fragrance; the *kacu* is a barely edible root that grows extremely vigorously.

12 Assailant's Ambition

Made to stitch garlands from morning to evening
The needle tires of such endless pricking.
She says in sadness, 'O jasmine-sister,
I pierce each day for the garland-maker
Thousands of flowers — but for so much hurt
To their softness and fragrance, what do I get?
Let *me* be a flower, dear God, in your kindness,
And pierce with beauty instead of sharpness!'
The jasmine sighs, 'O may it thus be:
Your wish be fulfilled, so that *I* can be free!'

13 Politics

Said the axe to the *sāl*-tree,[4] 'Do me a favour:
I have no shaft — please give me some timber!'
At once a shaft was made from a bough.
Did the axe have to act the beggar now?
He struck at the trunk with wild aggression.
The tree, poor thing, met total destruction!

14 Speaking Up for Yourself

A beautiful butterfly moans to a bee:
'Why does the poet not look at me?
My wings are so colourful; what have you got
That makes you poetic, while I am not?'
'You are,' said the bee, 'lovely indeed,
But you have no hum to make yourself heard.

---

4. A tall tree valuable for its hardwood and resin.

42

When I gather nectar, who doesn't know it?
I steal the heart of the flower *and* the poet.'

15. **The Stopping of Theft**
Queen Number One says, 'King, watch how
Your Queen Number Two is wheedling now!
Casting her out to live in the byre
Hasn't damped down her ambitious desire.
She hopes to persuade you with charming talk
To give her your best black cow to milk.'
'True,' says the king, 'but the girl's very cunning.
What can I do to stop her thieving?'
'One cure,' said the queen, 'will make it stop.
Give *me* the cow: *I'll* drink the milk up!'

16 **Self-enmity**
Bound hair and loose hair keep having rows.
A merry crowd gathers, amused by the noise.
Says bound hair, 'Loose hair, you're such a slob!'
Says loose hair, 'Bound hair, you're such a snob!'
'I hope you go bald,' says bound hair, sneering.
'I hope you get cut,' says loose hair, jeering.
The poet comes between them and says, 'Come on!
You are not two: you both are one!
You, bound hair, if loose hair were cut,
Would find yourself bald: what victory in that?'

17 **Emptied by Giving**
The empty cloud when the rains are over

Lingers on in the sky's far corner.
The rain-filled lake observes its plight,
Now and then smugly laughs at the sight.
Says, 'What a wretched, vain hanger-on!
It ought to call it a day and be gone.
Look at me, always so deep and full,
Nourishing, calming, steadfast, still.'
The cloud says, *'Bāpu,*[5] don't be so haughty.
Your watery depth redounds to *my* glory.'

18 Plain Speaking

The forest blooms with the coming of spring:
All that the *koel*-bird does is sing.
'I suppose,' says the crow, 'you've nothing to do
But flatter the spring with your hullabaloo.'
Pausing for a moment, the *koel* looks round:
'Who are you? Where do you come from, friend?'
'I'm the plain-speaking crow,' the crow replies.
'Delighted,' says the *koel*, and politely bows.
'Be free to speak plainly all the year long.
I'm happy with the truth of my own sweet song.'[6]

19 Heat's Price

A damp piece of timber tearfully moans:
'How bright are those sticks in the fire when it burns!

---

5. A somewhat patronising endearment, because the lake has been so patronising to the cloud.
6. The *koel* has a shrill, dominating call, rising up the scale, ending with a softer, cooing sound.

How can I get such warmth and brightness?'
Glumly he lies in a corner's darkness.
Say the burning sticks, 'O fresh green wood,
This fanciful envy will do you no good!
Do you think what we gain by being burned
Will fall unpaid-for into your hand?'
'Help,' says the timber, 'I don't want that!'
'Then wait,' say the sticks, 'for the beetles to bite.'

20 Humility

Said the wattle-fence, 'Grandfather bamboo,
Why do you bow as much as you do?
We're of the same race, yet you're always bending,
While we, though younger, keep proudly standing.'
He replied, 'It's to do with being so tall.
Bow down I must, for I cannot be small.'

21 Begging and Earning

'Why, O Earth, must you be so mean?
All this digging for a grain of corn!
Gifts should be cheerful, not so grudging.
Why such sweat and labour in farming?
What harm would it do you to give for no toil?'
Earth when she hears this says with a smile:
'That wouldn't increase my glory greatly,
And *your* pride and glory would vanish completely!'

22 The Need for Height

The flat field said in anger and pain:

'I fill the market with fruit and grain.
The mountain sits doing who knows what,
Like a great king perched on a throne of rock.
Why is God's management so unfair?
To me His reasons are not at all clear.'
'If all,' said the mountain, 'were flat and even,
How could rivers bring manna from heaven?'

23 Unconscious Mastery

'O Cloud, your breast is so full of water,
Yet when the wind blows you're such a fast runner.
You nurture a hundred fierce thunderstorms,
Yet eyes succumb to your cool blue charms.
How do you achieve this feat so easily?
I beg you, kindly explain this mystery.'
Rumbling with thunder, the cloud replies:
'I'm sorry, I see no cause for surprise.'

24 Power's Mercy

Narad the Sage[7] said, 'O Earth-mother,
Men eat your food, yet pay you with slander.
They call you muck, that ungrateful race;
They think of your soil as filthy and gross.
Let crops be shut down, let rain be cut off!
They'll soon understand what you are well enough.'
Said Earth with a smile, 'Oh let them whinge:
Do assaults so unequal merit revenge?

---

7. Narada is a mythological sage who is said to have invented the
   veena (lute) and composed some of the hymns in the *Rig-veda*.

Their slander leaves no mark on my head;
But if *I* got angry, they'd all drop dead.'

25 **Different Fulfilments**
The mango-branch says to the *bāblā*,[8] 'Friend,
Why must you come to so cruel an end?
Burnt in the stove, alas, to bits!'
Said the *bāblā*-branch, 'I've no regrets.
To be richly alive is your consummation.
Mine is achieved through self-immolation.'

26 **Toys**
The child imagines that when he's full grown
Every toy in the market will be his own.
To the man, however, such toys are trash:
Instead he is greedy for power and cash.
But surely he won't be truly grown-up
Till *all* lust for ownership comes to a stop.

27 **One-sided Calculation**
'If, twenty-seven, you were five times more,
My purse would be full, my wealth would soar.'
Said twenty-seven, 'That's fine with money,
But five times your *age* wouldn't be so funny.'

---

8. A kind of tree, only useful as firewood.

28 **Little Knowledge and More Knowledge**
The thirsty ass went to the lake's shore.
'Foul black water,' he said, and came back.
Said the water, 'To asses, water is black.
It's white to those who know a bit more.'

29 **Roots**
The treetop says, 'I'm high, you're low.'
The bottom of the tree says, 'Fine, who cares?
Because you're high, you take on airs.
My glory is, I've made *you* grow.'

30 **True Achievement**
The wasps said, 'Such a crowd of bees —
Is this small comb the best you can do?'
Said the bees, 'All right, *we* challenge *you*
To make a *smaller* honeycomb, please.'

31 **Outsider's Evaluation**
'Brother *mākāl*,'[9] the mango said,
'Once we were equal, here in the wood.
Men came along with *their* notions of good:
No more equality; pricing instead.'

32 **Contingent Relationship**
'Purse, my friend,' says the begging-bowl,
'You forget how closely related we are.'

---

9. The colocynth; an inedible fruit.

Says the purse, 'You'd want to keep *me* far
If *you* were the one who was stuffed full.'

33 Egalitarianism
The begging-bowl said, 'O *porte-monnaie,*
The difference between us is ever so tiny.
Let's do a deal.' The purse said crossly,
'Not while that difference stands in the way.'

34 Kinship-consciousness
The kerosene-lantern says to the taper,
'I'll wring your neck if you say we're kin.'
Whereas to the moon he says, 'Come in:
I welcome you warmly as my brother.'

35 Greatness of Spirit
A humble, nameless flower peeping
Out of a crack in the boundary-wall:
No one in the garden loves it at all.
But the sun says, 'Hi! How are you keeping?'

36 Seeing isn't Loving
The *jambu* [10] whispers, 'You say I'm swarthy,
Just because of that you look askance.
But why reject me, dear, with a glance?
Anyone who *eats* me knows I'm tasty.'

---

10. The *jambu*-tree produces a purplish-black astringent fruit in June and July.

37 **The Critic**
   Dud coin jeers at the humble rupee:
   'What are you worth? Just sixteen annas!'
   Rupee replies, 'That's more than your manners.
   Let one who has value criticise me.'

38 **Hating your Country**
   Worm to the soil: 'You're black and lowly.'
   Poet to the worm: 'But that's where you live!
   You eat what only the soil can give.
   It does you no credit to spurn it vilely.'

39 **Faith versus Zeal**
   Though her hands are empty, Faith is serene.
   Says Zeal, 'Please show your riches to me.'
   'They're within,' says Faith, 'there's nothing to see.'
   'Just look,' says Zeal, 'at the wealth *I* gain.'

40 **Old and Young**
   'Alas, you get more respect than I do,'
   Young hair complains to grey hair sadly.
   Says grey, 'You can have the respect gladly —
   Provided you make me as young as you.'

41 **Longing**
   'Mango, what life would suit you well?'
   'To be a sugarcane, straight and sweet.'
   'To *you,* sugarcane, what life's complete?'
   'A mango's: delicious to eat and smell.'

42 **Action's Errors**
Hair, on his high horse, says with a smirk,
'Arms and legs, how often you blunder!'
'O blameless hair,' they blithely answer,
'We make mistakes because we *work*.'

43 **Unbearably Good**
Says Best-I-can-do, 'O Better-still,
What heavenly realm does your radiance light?'
In tears he replies, 'The impotent spite
Of Envy surrounds me, where I dwell.'

44 **Canal's Grievance**
'Why, to make me, must labour be large,
When rivers dig themselves as they run?'
A courtier speaks: 'But you are the one
Who is *served* by the rivers, O *Mahārāj*.'[11]

45 **Arrogance**
A rocket boasts: 'Watch what I do!
I dare to hurl ash in the face of a star!'
'*That*,' says the poet, 'won't get you far.
The ash will fall back, right after you.'

46 **No Right to Mock**
The lamp laughs loud when the shooting-star drops:
'So poor an end to so grand a display!'

---

11. 'Great King'.

Night says, 'Good — keep laughing away,
Till your oil runs out and *your* light stops.'

47 Direct Evidence

Says the thunder, 'So long as I stay far off,
People don't know what I am: my booming
Is a cloud, they say; my blaze is lightning.
If I fall on their *heads,* they know well enough.'

48 Professional Difference

Nose says, 'Ears, your life must be poor.
No sense of smell, just earrings to wear.'
Ears say, 'Nose, how sad not to hear,
And all you can do in bed is *snore!*'

49 Poetry and Prose

'You're heavy, Club,' says the nimble dart.
'That's why you're always so stiff and straight.
Do what I do: cut through debate!
Instead of head-clobbering, pierce the heart.'

50 Vying for Devotion

Chariot-festival — thousands enthused:
Rolling on the road in wild adoration.
Wagon, road, image: in each the conviction:
'I'm a god, I'm a god!' True God is amused.[12]

---

12. The most famous Hindu chariot-festival is at Puri in Orissa, when
     an image of Jagannath ('Lord of the World', a name for Vishnu)
     is carried on a huge cart to be bathed in the sea.

51 **Humble Pride**
Says the moss to the pond, 'Don't ever forget —
A drop of my dew helps to make *you* wet.'

52 **Cause for Doubt**
The fake diamond says, 'How big I am!'
That is how we know you're a sham.

53 **Free to be Low**
When you're down in the mud you can sling it about.
Those still above it had better watch out!

54 **Revelation**
Love asks eyes that are tearful and wordless,
'Who are you?' They answer, 'Gratefulness.'

55 **Ungratefulness**
Echo mocks Noise lest others discover
How deeply Echo is Noise's debtor!

56 **Futile Effort**
Can those with no power to make themselves taller
Really belittle those who are greater?

57 **Good and Bad**
Says the net, 'I'm not lifting mud any longer!'
'Then you won't,' says the fisherman, 'catch fish either.'

58 **The Same Path**
Let's shut the door to block out sin!
'Then how', says Truth, 'shall I get in?'

59 **Immutability**
However you turn and turn about,
Your left hand is left and your right hand is right.

60 **The Art of Abuse**
'Too thin!' says the *lāṭhi* to the walking-stick.
The stick sneers back, 'Too short and thick!'[13]

61 **Scandal-monger**
Mud, you sully everyone's purity.
But doesn't that simply make *you* dirty?

62 **Fine Distinction**
Favour laments, 'I give and get nothing.'
Compassion says, 'No charge for my giving.'

63 **Public and Private**
'I've given my light to the world,' says the moon.
'Any blots that I have are mine alone.'

64 **Prudent Mediocrity**
The finest are happy to walk with the lowly.
Those in between are not so friendly.

---

13. A *lāṭhi* is a short stick used as a baton or truncheon.

65 **Glory in Enmity**
The blind owl boasts whenever he can:
'Do you know who my enemy is? The sun!'

66 **One-upmanship**
'I am,' says Time, 'this world's Creator.'
'Then I,' says the clock, 'am Creation's maker!'

67 **Ephemeral and Eternal**
When Kings assert that the laws they fashion
Create what is just, Justice replies:
'New kinds of *in*justice are what you devise.
I'm old. How can I be freshly begotten?'

68 **Humble Gift**
Says the desert, 'O Cloud, I'm ever-failing:
For the water you give, what can I give back?'
Says the cloud, 'Don't worry, there's nothing I lack.
You give me, dear friend, the joy of giving.'

69 **Fog's Complaint**
'Why,' says Fog, 'when the clouds remain
So remote, and I stay close, is their merit
With you the greater?' 'You,' says the poet,
'Are a trickster: clouds bring cooling rain.'

70 **Taking and Giving**
Hands say, 'Cynic, you're wrong to say
We're only cupped when we want to receive;

We're also cupped when we want to *give*.
We're filled with *offerings* when we pray.'

71 **Useful Uselessness**
O cropless Sea, what is your worth?
Idly dancing through half our world!
Says the Sea, 'If my space were usefully filled,
Who'd suck rivers from the breasts of the earth?'

72 **The Fragrance of Loss**
The fragrance flees from the flower, alas;
The flower plaintively calls it back.
'Come come', says the breeze, 'its loss is no lack:
You wouldn't *have* scent if it didn't pass.'

73 **Submission**
The rising sun outshines the moon,
Yet the calm-faced moon still lingers there:
'I wait,' she says, 'on the western shore,
To salute the sunrise before I'm gone.'

74 **Mutual Appreciation**
Says Word to Work, 'When I see you in action
I feel so ashamed of my emptiness!'
Says Work, 'But Word, my shame is no less:
It's you, not I, who achieves perfection.'

75 **Stronger than Strength**
A raging storm: who wins the battle?
In the end, a breeze, soft and gentle.

76 **Acceptance of Duty**
'Who'll do my work?' says the setting sun.
The world of Nature offers no answer.
A clay-lamp speaks: 'O Lord and Master,
I'm willing to do what little I can.'

77 **Pointless Grief**
Weeping at night won't bring back the sun,
And it makes the light of the stars seem vain.

78 **Delusion**
Left bank sighs and moans with despair:
'My pleasure is all on the other side.'
Right bank's moans are equally loud:
'All my delight is over there.'

79 **Flower and Fruit**
Flower shouts loudly, 'Where, O Fruit,
Have you got to now? You stray so far!'
Fruit says, 'Sir, I'm right where *you* are.
Why shout? I'm always here in your heart.'

80 **Shallow and Deep**
'O mighty sea, you're dark and obscure,'
Says the pot of water. 'I'm clear and bright.'
Truth observes, 'You may talk straight,
But the silence of depth can say far more.'

81 **Beyond all Questioning**
'What, O sea, is the language you speak?'
'A ceaseless question,' the sea replies.
'What does your silence, O Mountain, comprise?'
'A constant non-answer,' says the peak.

82 **Freedom**
The arrow thinks, 'I fly, I'm free,
Unlike the wretched, restricted bow.'
Bow laughs and says, 'But don't you know,
Your freedom, arrow, is subject to me!'

83 **Fruitless Abuse**
Silk-cotton flower, rejected, by all,
Calmly listens, then says with a smile:
'Silently, while they sneer and rail
My beauty blossoms, complete and full.'

84 **Rapture's Anxiety**
Young bud wakes and raptly surveys
This fresh green Earth, full of scent and sound;
Cries out, 'O darling World all around,
Stay close by till the end of my days!'

85 **Praise and Censure**
True Worth is asked by Praise and Censure,.
'Which of us counts as your friend, dear sir?'
'My friends and enemies both you are,'
Says Worth. 'I pay no attention to either.'

86 **Closer than Kinship**
Ash says, 'Fire is my own close brother.'
Smoke says, 'Yes, but I'm his twin.'
Firefly says, 'I'm not his kin —
But compared to you both, I'm even closer.'

87 **Primary Mystery**
Flute remarks, 'On my own I'm empty.
A puff is needed to make me sound.'
Puff says, 'Yes, but I'm just wind.
To us both, the player remains a mystery.'

88 **Invisible Agency**
By turning buds into flowers, Night
Secretly fills the forest, then goes.
The awakening flowers say, 'Dawn, we're yours.'
Dawn says gladly, 'No quarrel with that.'

89 **Truth's Discipline**
Says Fancy to Truth, 'I'm not like you.
I'm free, not endlessly chained and bound.'
Says Truth, 'That's why you're so unsound.
The rules that shackle me make me true.'

90 **Beauty's Discipline**
Says Man, 'Come on, be brave, go for it!'
Says Woman, 'Really! Whatever next?'
'Why,' says Man, 'are your steps so fixed?'
'Therein her beauty,' comments the poet.

91 **The Pain of Being Great**
Calumny makes the sun feel sorrowful.
'What can I do to be loved by all?'
'Give up,' says God, 'your solar role.
Do an easier job to please a handful.'

92 **Attachment and Detachment**
Love says, 'Detachment, your creed's untrue.'
'But you,' says Detachment, 'are sunk in delusion.
Shed selfishness, seek your own liberation!'
'In that case,' says Love, 'I'm the same as you.'

93 **Rest**
Work and rest belong to each other —
Like eye and eyelid linked together.

94 **Life**
Birth and death, taking turns, make life's game:
Alternating up and down feet do the same.

95 **Unchangeable**
So what if one thing becomes another!
What's here *in toto* remains, my friend.
If sorrows could all be brought to an end
We'd quickly discover sorrow in pleasure.

96 **Unstealable**
Thieves want my gold, Death wants my son,
All I possess is desired by Fate.

Slanderers want to steal my repute —
But my joy as a poet eludes every one.

97 **Pleasure and Pain**
Jasmine, knocked flat by torrential rain,
Cries, 'Who's shooting such arrows of death?'
Says rain, 'My blessings descend to earth:
Some find it pleasant; others complain.'

98 **The Driver**
I inquire of Fate: 'Who can it be,
So cruelly, ruthlessly driving me on?'
'Look round,' Fate says. I stop and turn:
The driver behind is my previous Me.

99 **Discovery of Truth**
Says Mother Earth, 'When daylight's shining,
Nothing other than *me* shows.
At night when I'm hidden the sky displays
The Eternal World's resplendent writing.'

100 **The Best Time**
Dark heavy rain of grief has come.
O brother farmer, don't sit at home.
Dry heart has turned to rain-soft loam.
Sow your seeds: it's the best time.

101 **Double-dealing**
The World — that enchantress — said to me:
'Our love will keep us eternally bound.'

Then said, when our dealings came to an end:
'You forgot that you would one day be free.'

102 Willing to be Cheated

'O World', says the Hero, 'I know what you are.
Do not suppose your tricks can deceive me.
I give what I give you entirely deliberately:
Cheat if you will — I'll give you far more.'

103 Clear Truth

Says the World, 'I always play with you straight:
Birth-and-death, joy-and-sorrow, all quite clear.
Whatever I say is true and fair.
It's you who fail to interpret it right.'

104 Beginning and End

Says End, 'O Beginning, your pride is vain.
Everything comes to an end in time.'
'Brother,' says Beginning, 'no end can come
Without a beginning dawning again.'

105 Disrobing

'I've vanquished the world,' cries fearsome Death.
Life keeps trying its best to disrobe him.
Whatever the stripping, God still protects him:
Increases non-stop the supply of cloth!

106 Eternal Renewal

Night tells Day, tenderly kissing:
'Death though I am, I'm your mother too.

Don't be afraid: what I kill I renew.
I give fresh life to you every morning.'

107 Death

If, O Death, you were formless and empty,
There'd be straightaway no trace of the world.
You are full and complete: hence you can hold
The world in your lap, rock it like a baby.

108 Power behind Power

Eyesight boasts of its power to see
By day, but at night dissolves into tears.
To Light it says: 'I now realize
I see even *you* thanks to you, not me.'

109 Fundamental Reality

'Small though I am,' says Light's spark,
'What can be independent of me?
Yet when I blink, behind me I see
You, O first, beginningless Dark.'

110 Similar Achievements

'Star,' says *śephāli*, 'I've shed my flowers.'
'My work,' says the star, 'is also complete.
We've filled the departing basket of Night
With white petals and the sky's fires.'[14]

---

14. The white flowers of the *śephāli*-tree bloom mainly in autumn, opening at night and falling at dawn.

Jottings
(Lekhan, 1927)

1.

My dreams are gems of sparkling life,
      Fireflies flitting;
In the still depths of the dark night,
    Light's particles darting.

2.

My jottings are brief
    As a roadside flower
That passers-by see
    But do not remember.

3.

A moth counts not by years,
    But moment by moment:
So the time it has is sufficient.

4.

Dreams are nests that birds
    In sleep's obscure recesses
Build from our talkative days'
    Discarded bits and pieces.

5.

My work's heaviest freight
Will sink from its own weight.
Perhaps these words that are lighter
Will continue to grace the water.

6.

How wantonly Spring's breeze
    Throws the bud's petals away —
Forgetful of future fruit,
    Thrilled with a moment's play!

7.

A spark is fulfilled
    By its momentary flight:
To soar and then die
    Is its whole delight.

8.

    The tree stares down
At the beautiful shade beneath it.
    The shade is its own,
Yet it cannot itself possess it.

9.

May love, like the sun's brightness,
By giving you glorious liberty
Hold you within its compass.

10.
From the sleeping earth,
    Delight is released;
Rushes through the leaves:
    A rustling gust.

11.
Night is a bottomless ocean,
    Dark and immeasurable.
Day floats along on its surface:
    A colourful bubble!

12.
My gifts are too shy to be sure
    That any will recall them.
Perhaps in your kindness therefore
    You will remember them.

13.
Spring, like a child,
Paints colours in the dust;
Rubs them out and moves on:
    Her pictures are lost.

14.
Crowds of worshippers come to pray:
    The deity's thoughts stray
To the yard of the temple where children play.

15.
Your oleanders are white;
    Mine are red.
The silent eyes
Of Springtime lovers
    Waking together,
    Knowing each other.

16.
Sky holds earth in its firm embrace
Despite being parted by infinite space.

17.
The far came close: when day was over,
Though it went away, it was even closer.

18.
    O endless dark,
To help this lamp's shy spark
    Overcome its fears,
Light up numberless stars!

19.
May my speech emerge from hiding
    Like a moth in the fading light:
    Take its last occasion for flight
And lose itself, wings humming!

20.

The mountain-top soars,
      Hidden in cloud,
Ignoring the lake's appeal.
Anxious beauty implores
At the feet of one too detached
      To move or feel.

21.

Clouds of the morning floating,
Light and shadow playing,
      Like somebody passing the time
      With a smiling childish game.

22.

That cloud is a vaporous mountain,
      That mountain looks like a cloud.
Recurring age after age in the dreams of Time,
      What is this mood?

23.

God desires that his temples be built from love.
Men raise brick-built towers to the sky above.

24.

Said the wind to the flame,
      'You're mine, by right.'
But just when he thought he had won,
      His claim was snuffed out.

71

25.

The ocean keeps the shores asunder,
　　But gives them a tearful song
To express their bottomless love for each other.

26.

He who lights the lamps of the stars
Watches each lamp on earth that appears.

27.

　　In my songs, O Lord,
　　　　Your touch I feel,
Like a mountain's touch on the sea
　　　　Through a waterfall.

28.

Dawn is a many-hued flower
　　That fades away
To produce a pure white fruit:
The sun's majestic power.

29.

Darkness is like a lovesick bride,
　　Her face veiled by her sari.
She waits for the absent light to return,
　　Watches the road keenly.

30.

O flower of mine, do not become
    A foolish fop's possession:
Receive instead at your life's dawn
       My benediction.

31.

Life's game is so keen and fast
Its playthings, one by one,
Break, and are left in the past.

32.

    O crescent moon,
       Late is your rising;
But the perfumed flowers of the night
       Are still longing.

33.

The wind is up, the sails tug,
    But the anchor is stuck in the mud.
Ashamed at being unable to find it,
    The boat wants to hide its head.

34.

The sky's blue stares
    At the woodland green.
The wistful breeze
    Sighs in between.

35.

Pity the worm, O flower:
　　It is not a bee.
Forlorn it feels at its love's
　　　　Futility.

36.

　　Because it knows it can expect
　　　　The kiss of flame at night,
The lamp accepts the day's long neglect.

37.

Pain that by day is covered and gagged by the sun
Shows in the dark, when the stars' fires burn.

38.

These veena-strings of mine,
Ashamed to be out of tune
　　Beg for a song.
Don't desert them for long![1]

39.

In a nest, silent and shadowy,
　　That is ours alone,
Speechless, secret agony
　　Dwells on its own.

1.　The veena (*vīṇā*) is a lute-like instrument. See fn.7, p.46.

40.

    Light,
When it tenderly
Garlands the dark,
    Is Creativity.

41.

    The memory
That Shade retains
Of Light in his heart
       Is Art.

42.

When Spring runs riot through the flowers,
    Love's wine thrills us.
At the end of our blossoming days,
    Love's food fulfils us.

43.

    The day is gone.
I sit and listen in the silent dark
    To the knock, knock
    At the door of my heart
Of my frail, wandering hopes
    Preparing to return
       At dawn.

44.

Children play on the crumbled victory-portal,
    Constructing a den from the rubble.

45.

You've squandered your wealth, O cloud,
    On your passion for colour:
Called to the moon's *salon*,   ·
    You've nothing to offer.

46.

Ragged dusty feathers lie,
Forgetful of how they flew in the sky.

47.

    Delay on my journey:
    This cherry-blossom fell
Before I could give it to you.
But *your* gift, how it cheers me!
    This azalea's smile
Shows I have not upset you.

48.

When I wandered into your garden,
    There were two buds there.
In the spring breeze, when I'm gone,
    They will burst into flower.

49.

O mighty ocean, how you lure
The heart of man to wild adventure!
Your endless story of awesome fear
Tempts him to face colossal danger!

50.

In sky beyond sky, in land beyond land, the sun
    Is born to new dawns, again and again.

51.

The firefly carefully scours the dust.
For him, the stars do not exist.

52.

I receive for my work
    God's fair estimation. .
I receive for my songs
    His tender affection.

53.

I brought as my present to you
    Just one of my flowers.
Alas, you want my whole garden:
    Take it — it's yours.

54.

Spring, you've come to this place in error,
    It seems to me.

If so, please leave at least one flower
    On the wizened tree.

55.

'I'll never forget you,' said the rose,
    Gazing into the eyes
        Of the morning sun.
A moment later, her petals had gone.

56.

No trace of my flight
    Shows in the sky,
But what a delight
    It was to fly!

57.

The timid shadow deep in the wood
    Adores the light.
When the flowers are told this by the leaves,
    They smile with delight.

58.

The smile of God in the stars in the sky at night
Is brought to earth by a firefly's fleeting light.

59.

The mist may seem to throw the mountain into obscurity,
But nothing can shake its grand, unmoving majesty!

60.

The hills stare at the sky, but they have no speech.
Oh earth's dumb longing for that which is out of reach!

61.

When once you gave me, Beauty,
    A sharp-thorned flower,
I smiled and thanked you gladly.

62.

Know, my friend, you haven't incurred
Any debt through being loved by me.
        Love is its own reward.

63.

Small is not small, it can cover the vast:
A handful of people are more than a host.

64.

When Truth hears in music
    Its own voice,
A smile blooms
    On Beauty's face.

65.

A kiss from the sky has made
    My flowers bloom with pleasure.
A lover's touch is displayed,
    But not the actual lover.

66.

The bubble confines itself to its own sphere.
Ignorant of the sea, it bursts into thin air.

67.

Oh vanished life together!
    Let longing, day and night,
    Keep memory's lamp alight
With fire that will last forever.

68.

    When the sky is grey,
The grieving clouds forget
    That they themselves
Have blotted the sunshine out.

69.

When God comes and begs at mankind's door,
We understand how truly rich we are.

70.

The perfect player looks for an instrument that will suit.
    The player, meanwhile, is sought by a perfect flute.

71.

The day of the very first flowers on earth
Was the day my songs were called to birth.

72.

To try to perfect the world is an act of oppression.
Selfless Utopians cause the most destruction.

73.

The universe is forever changing
Like surf on an ocean breaking and foaming
Whose depths are bottomless, calm and unmoving.

74.

When we've paid in full for a new existence,
We are free to enjoy it, without any hindrance.

75.

By twisting it too hard,
    The bully spoils the key.
In the end he must use an axe
    To assert his authority.

76.

Birth is release from mysterious dark night
Into day's still more mysterious stream of light.

77.

The songs in my heart
Are a flock of birds
    Whose eager quest
Finds in your voice
    A nest that is best.

78.

Gifts you give me whimsically,
Gaily and ephemerally,
Shooting-star-like, blazing briefly,
Fire the autumn dark within me!

79.

Off it goes!
Away it floats!
　　The lazy load
　　Of my idle hours
　　In my playfully made
Paper-boats.

80.

When Spring appears in Winter's yard too early,
　　It soon withdraws.
The mango-buds that rushed to greet it gladly
　　Are left to freeze.

81.

　　O Love,
By forgiving all hurt
The punishment you exert
　　Is formidable.
　　　　O Beauty,
Your silent pain
At the harsh blows you sustain
　　Is unbearable.

82.

Divine Creation
   Is born anew
At the World's destruction.
The work of the devil
   Is smashed by the weight
Of its own evil.

83.

The tree was planted recently;
   Its flower is very old;
It brings the ancient story
   Its first seed told.

84.

My love these days
Aimlessly weaves
   Through the empty air.
Home is there none
   In a nest left bare
By a love that is gone.

85.

Each champak-flower brings
A message unchangeable
From time immemorial![2]

---

2.   The long, golden-yellow flowers of the champak (*cãpā*) tree bloom
   in summer and are compared by poets to beautiful tapering fingers.

86.

Fiery the path that grief must burn
    To a place beyond all pain.

87.

    Now that you've gone,
    Leaving me alone,
Whose touch is this I feel in the sky's blue?
When in the woods and winds and grasses,
A trembling hint of a movement passes,
    Who is it? You?

88.

Dawn, all alone at the door of the dark,
    Plucks her veena.
But when the sun rises she pulls down her veil
    And is there no longer.

89.

To dew, the sun
    Is only knowable
Deep within
    A droplet's spherical.

90.

Fenced in by its own unfettered sterility
The desert is imprisoned for all eternity.

91.

From the sacrificial fire of the earth,
　　　Flames rise
　　In the form of trees:
The sparks that are scattered are flowers.

92.

　　　Daylight fades.
　　Now it's the sky's turn
　　To meditate on the sun,
Using the stars as rosary-beads.

93.

My daily work receives its fee each day;
My love desires supreme, eternal pay.

94.

Work can expect each day the pay that is due;
I must wait for Love's supreme reward to accrue.

95.

Night's language is understood by Day:
　　But what does the fog say?

96.

　　An unknown flower
Calls out to the travelling poet:
'The land that is mine, my friend,
　　Do you not also know it?'

97.

The book-chewing bug
    Thinks people are fools.
How can they not know
    That books are meals?

98.

Why do our thoughts keep dwelling on future fruits?
Let flowers on the branch suffice to gladden our hearts!

99.

In the cloudy sky today I seem to see
    Shade on the brow of Eternity,
Cast when the King of the Gods feels misery.

100.

In the sunset's crimson light
    The earth is like
    A ripened fruit
That the hands of the dark night
    Reach out to pluck.

101.

The butterfly need do no more
    Than love the lotus.
The bee gathering honey all year round
    Must be more industrious.

102.

Mist traps Dawn
    In a baffling net:
Blind and bound,
    She cannot get out.

103.

Thinks the morning star:
    'For me and no other
The sun rises radiantly.'
'That's fine,' says Dawn, 'by me'.

104.

The boundless space of the sky
        Stays wide and empty,
So that earth can imagine there
    Pictures of immortality.

105.

The jasmine bud is not ashamed to be tiny:
Fullness reigns in its heart, invisibly.
Muffled though Spring's speech may be by such confining,
Beauty smiles at being so beautifully held back from flowering!

106.

Flowers are words: the leaves around them
Are the layers of silence that surround them.

107.

If Evening can forgive the sins of the day,
  Peace will come her way.

108.

Love unites through the power of attraction;
Power must use the chains of oppression.

109.

The burden of years
That great tree bears
Seems as light
As an instant's weight.

110.

My pilgrimage does not aim at the end of the road.
My thoughts are set on the shrines on either side.

111.

How to describe your smile, my love:
  So sweet and pure,
Like the scent of an unknown flower!

112.

The more we honour the dead excessively
The more we exaggerate Death's supremacy.

113.

Futile the tears of the shore chasing
The wind in the sails of the boat crossing!

114.

Because it encounters
    Beauty there,
Truth loves its borders.

115.

Lord Shiva dances in new expressions of beauty,
    In the flowers of spring and fields of crops rippling.
    In you too, Gauri, he is endlessly dancing,
In your sweet expressions of heart, mind and body.[3]

116.

Day places its golden veena
    In the silent hands of the stars,
To be tuned to Eternity's raga.

117.

Faith is a bird at dawn
    Whose song says, 'Light, light!'
Before night's dark is gone.

118.

Evening empties the cup of Day and throws it
      Into the yard of the stars.
Washing it clean with darkness, Night refills it
    With new nectar that Dawn supplies.

---

3.   Gauri is a name for Durga or Parvati, Shiva's consort.

119.

Let my love, in my work by day, find energy;
Then, in the night, find deep peace and harmony.

120.

Those flowers of dawn that have gone,
    Deserting the day's light,
At dusk come back again,
    Dressed as the stars of the night.

121.

Let go of what must go!
    It will cause you hurt
If you do not open the door
        To let it out.

122.

The shore when the tide is high
    Softly asks of the sea,
'The words that your waves would say,
    Please write them down for me.'
But their eagerly scribbling foam
    Gives the sea no satisfaction.
Line after line must succumb
    To ever-impatient correction.

123.

The inner treasure
That lasts forever

Of the Old, O New,
Has been brought by you.

124.

The earth looks up at the midnight moon and muses,
    'What language is this she speaks,
    When she wordlessly smiles and gazes?'

125.

There's a still centre the circle cannot find,
However much it dances round and round.

126.

A day-time lamp is only there
      To keep oil in store.
A night-time lamp gives light.
    To compare the two is unfair.

127.

The mountain keeps its snow to itself:
    Heavy the load it bears.
But the world must carry the molten streams
      The mountain pours.

128.

Our being so close
    Is a kind of screen.
Pierce it with your love
    So that I can be seen.

129.

O listen, listen
To the buds in the woods whose cries
    To the sun say, 'Open,
        Open our eyes!'

130.

The joy that was held in gaol
    Deep in the earth
Has emerged in this fig-tree's fresh green leaves.
    In the freedom of the wind for a while
        It revels and lives:
From dark still dreams, a whirling brilliant birth!

131.

The toys with which I've idly
    Filled this paper boat,
        Are my memories.
If one morning it turns up at your *ghāṭ*,[4]
    Use them for *your* frivolities!

132.

When under the night the daylight disappears,
Then, in the dark's bright meditating eyes,
    It burns as a hundred million stars.

---

4.   A *ghāṭ* is a mooring-place for a boat, or steps down to a pond or
     river for bathing or washing.

133.

Let lightless, hopeless, merciless outer pain
Be healed by the limitless light that shines within!

134.

Like a lotus of light, the setting sun
    Has closed its petals up.
    Let it bloom in a new tongue,
    With new unfaltering hope,
    On the shore of a new dawn!

135.

In your book of life so many pages are empty.
Fill them with what your own mind fashions inwardly.
    Let the secret poet there
    Give you *your* picture of heaven:
Let his godlike message touch your imagination.

136.

    God desires to wear
    A garland made by mankind;
Which is why his own basket of flowers
    Is left in the lap of the soil
        For us to find.

137.

The *mallikā*-bud[5] looks up at the sun and muses,
'When will I be as big a flower as he is?'

---

5.   Arabian jasmine.

138.
Sun, discard your ornaments!
Let the boat of the evening clouds
Carry away your crown.
Go down
To the temple where Death resides
To make your obeisance
In silence.

139.
My evening lamp offers
Namaskārs[6]
To the night's stars.

140.
Stitched by autumn's grass-tip needles,
This necklace of dew will quickly pass;
Yet it's sure of a permanent place
In Beauty's annals.
Not so a king's necklace of jewels
Whose lustre steadily dwindles.

141.
That which, during the day, I slighted,
Has become my lamp, now night has started.

---

6. Hindu greeting: the word *namaskār(a)* is said, accompanied by the
folding of the hands in a prayer-like position.

142.
When it falls to the ground, the petal is sure
That Spring won't come to the earth any more.

143.
   O breeze in Spring,
   Have you forgotten
The friendship of flowers is best?
    You wander along
    The streets of the town,
      Just raising dust.

144.
O unknown friend
When I look in your eyes
Whom do I see?
    That glance,
Hidden in darkness
For thousands of years,
Yet somehow familiar to me.

145.
Breeze from the south, you've come to awaken the flowers.
Back you will go to the south, when the garden clears.

146.
O flock of ducks in the wind in winter,
The wine of flight inspires your wings!
    Ecstatic with dreams of remoteness,

Drunk with the sky's blueness,
Tell me, how can I fill my songs
With that same liquor?

147.

Why is the dew-soaked forest's rustling
So unsettling?
As if in the early morning
It disturbs with its whispering
A nameless Beloved's dreaming.

148.

Smearing the brow of evening
With the sun's sandal-paste hues,
Sky-goddesses, silently weeping,
Cover their eyes.

149.

When He who is silent lowers his Word
Into what I say,
Then I know both Him and myself
In the same way.

150.

In my thorns, my errors lie,
Not in my flowers.
Let the thorns, my darling, be mine:
The flowers are yours.

151.

I see there at your window
    Your lamp's immobile light.
Who knows what tune it plays
    On the veena of deep night?

152.

Oh why this woodland message brought by the breeze
    To the ears of the homesick city trees?

153.

O forest-wanderer,
    My *bakul*-flower[7] says,
    'I know you well'
To your cherry-flower.

154.

This sumptuous palace is a ravenous demon
    Whose arms are tied by the weight of possessions;
I recall how its rooms were once empty and poor,
    And arms were free for the heart's affections.

155.

That cloud floating around so high
Expresses the mountain's longing to fly.

156.

That which I have gained from afar
Is closer to me than what is near.

---

7. See fn.3, p.41.

157.

From the ocean's heaving depths, a plea
Wells up to the silent sky: 'Kiss me!'

158.

'Listen,' says the moon,
   'O morning star,
When night is departing
   Why oh why
Do you now appear
   With a smile so bright?
The way you slip in
   Between darkness and light
      Is very confusing!'

159.

Those profligate, worthless clouds!
   The gold they got from the dawn
   By the end of the day has gone.
    They float off, all serene.

160.

I thought I would count the stars —
   My counting went on all night.
But I kept on losing the thread.
   This morning I've understood
     That only by not
     Looking too closely,
   Do we see a whole thing right.

Just *look* at the sea—
Don't drive yourself crazy
Trying to scoop it out!

161.

I thought I knew you in my heart, my love,
But maybe I did not.
You kept some things to yourself, because
Your feelings were hurt.

162.

I've made you into a garland,
Lilies, thinking you are my own.
Why are you still so foreign?

163.

You looked at that early flowering tree
Thinking only of fruit.
In vain its flowers bloomed and fell
One Phalgun night.[8]

164.

The shade of my tree is offered to those
Who come and go
Fleetingly.
Its fruit matures for somebody whose
Coming I watch for
Constantly.

---

8.   Phalgunā (*Phālgun*) is the first month of Spring, mid-February to mid-March.

165.

When fire is held captive
   Inside the tree,
Leaves, flowers, fruits arise.
When it wildly, brazenly breaks its bonds
   It just makes ashes and dies.

166.

The garden presents its flowers to the moon.
The sea has none to give, so it feels forlorn.

167.

The pen doesn't know whose fingers hold it,
And the words it writes mean nothing to it.

168.

In blaming the bad, you spare no word.
Why be so chary of praising the good?

169.

Moon isn't trapped by sky by force.
It binds itself to its own course.

170.

Light's greatness,
   Filling the sky,
     Sees
   If it can also squeeze
Into a dewdrop's smallness.

171.

In the razor-blade,
    What glittering scorn,
Mocking the light
    Of the sun at dawn!

172.

One alone is empty: it has nothing to support it.
It only starts to find itself when one is added to it.

173.

Accept you're not the same, if you want two to be one.
Differences increase, if you try to break them down.

174.

Death's creed is One;
Life's creeds are Many.
The death of God leads
To the worship of uniformity.

175.

Darkness regards the One as single;
Light sees it from every varied angle.

176.

Let the thorns of a flower be seen
By those with an eye for flowers:
    Not by others.

177.

If you kick the dust, it'll fly in your eyes and face.
Spray it with water: its nuisance will vanish apace.

178.

For the constantly active, keen do-gooder,
Where to *be* good is the time and leisure?

179.

One who would *do* good is never asked to stay.
One who just *is* good is never turned away.

180.

If you cripple him yourself, to take him on your shoulder,
It won't sound very sweet to him to call this a favour.

181.

Maybe you've got work, or maybe you lack it,
But don't, brother, make such a song and dance about it!

182.

Work is our duty, that's quite true.
But shame on those who only think
    Of work they must do.

183.

Work and leisure
Play together;
Waves play a game
With the ocean's calm.

184.
The stamp of Death
    Gives value to living;
    Hence in our giving
Of life, there is worth.

185.
Where feeling is lacking,
    Spikes are all you get:
Plants in the desert
    Are thorny and squat.

186.
What I see in the mirror is my image, not me:
How strangely deluded to be proud of what I see!

187.
If you want to be bigger than you are,
To your own self humbly bow.

188.
When a man treats love as a business proposition,
Love takes a backseat view of the action.

189.
When Love makes sorrow its crowning jewel,
I discover the Joy of Love for real.

190.
The truth that's immortal, beyond all measure,
Is proven by Death, over and over.

Sparks

(Sphuliṅga, 1945)

1.

Keep clearing rubbish from the yard of the temple:
    Sweep away the ephemeral.

2.

I've never stopped thirsting,
    Searching and travelling,
    Spun so many words,
    Taken on such loads.
    Must I keep questing
    For what I'm still lacking?
Must the pain of unsung songs
Keep breaking my veena's strings?[1]

3.

I have made many garlands
For morning guests to wear.
    Now in the evening,
    Who is this here?
Alas, must I make her a garland
From leaves withered and sere?

---

1.   See fn.7, p.46.

4.

Bringing a message from beyond the dark
  The rising sun speaks out;
  Reveals the marvels of the world
  By its single enveloping light.

5.

The plough cuts the earth for its fruit.
From the scratches of pen on paper
Come the produce of mind and heart.

6.

  When it bursts into flower
The creeper's pride has no end —
As if it has received a letter
  In the sky's own hand.

7.

  The night is over:
  In the room's dark corner
Snuff out the smoke-black light.
  In the eastern sky
  On this festive day
The lamp of the world shines bright.
  May all who proceed
  Along the same road
Perceive each other aright.

8.

Heart that feels without thinking,
    What are you doing —
Tearfully searching the stars
    For fallen flowers?

9.

Like pure clear water
    May your life flow along;
May your path be joyous
    With songs you will sing.
The further the fuller,
Growing like a river,
May both banks garner
    The gifts you will bring.

10.

Like a flute playing in the sky
    A message from the not-known.
Animals do not hear it;
    People try to catch the tune.

11.

Keeping each other company
The lights those two stars carry
Will unite in the temple of Eternity.

12.

Golden clouds in the sky
Paint pictures without end:
But they don't leave their names behind.

13.

Sky's light quietly hides
    Under the earth:
Until at the call of Spring
    Flowers give it birth.

14.

At the height of its burning
    The fire's flaming
Warned me itself to keep clear.
    Now that it's fading,
    Cooling and dying
Its ashes are what I fear.
Let me not stray too near.

15.

    We make today
    The house where we play:
Tomorrow its charms will have passed.
    Our games in the dust
    Are erased by dust.

16.

The flower doesn't understand
    The worth of its beauty.

What it so easily gained
    It gives away easily.

17.

Behind your own locked door
    Darkness reigns.
Open your eyes to where outside
    Perpetual light shines.

18.

When you give yourself truly and fully
You encounter an image of beauty.

19.

Hiding in the shade of trees,
    The flower confers
Its scent on the southern breeze.

20.

A new year starts:
It wants in its ledgers
Youthful accounts —
Not an old codger's.
But I have some hope
I'm not yet finished,
That newness within me
Isn't quite vanished —
For equally old
Is that champak-tree,[2]

---

2. See fn.2, p.83.

Yet still its blooms
    Smell heavenly.

21.

The love in my body and heart
For the earth's shadow and light
    Has stayed over years.
With its cares and its hopes it has thrown
    A language of its own
    Into blue skies.
It lives in my joys and glooms,
In the Spring night's buds and blooms,
    Like a *rākhi*-band
    On the Future's hand.[3]

22.

Come, Spring, come here!
Wake the grace of the flower
In the peaceful room where it's hid —
The secret heart of the bud.
Let the leaves by your delicate brush
    Be dabbed with colour.
Let your promise of fruits to come
    Be brought like a letter.

---

3.   A *rākhi* is a thread worn round the wrist. As part of the campaign against Lord Curzon's decision, in 1905, to partition Bengal, Tagore initiated a *rākhi-bandhan* ('thread-tying') ceremony as a symbol of Hindu-Muslim unity and the unity of Bengal.

23.

Light comes by day;
Darkness is brought by night.
In the Sea of Death, the two together,
　　Yamuna, Ganga,
　　Black and white.[4]

24.

Light never leaves
　　Footprints in the air.
Because it knows when to go,
　　It's always there.

25.

Let Life's star gleam
　　With hope's light.
　　Let its rays stream
Through the coming night.

26.

　　Up and down roads
　　From dawn to dark,
　　Motley crowds
Cry and laugh as they walk.
　　They want to leave a mark
　　Of their names in the dust:

4.　At the sacred *saṅgam* (confluence) of the Jumna (*Yamunā*) and
Ganges *(Gaṅgā)* at Allahabad, a contrast between the colours of the
two rivers can be clearly seen.

But before the day's passed
    When the dust has blown
    The lines will be gone.

27.

We see God's face in the light of the smile
    Of brother to brother.
We worship God when our hearts are full
    Of love for each other.

28.

Wave, you dance so wildly!
Wind, you blow so keenly!
    Boat no longer knows
    Which way it goes.

29.

This banyan and fig-tree grove
    Embodies devotion.
Its massed shadows instil
    Deep meditation.
A detached breeze in its leaves
    Inspires adoration.

30.

I worship a value that is so supreme,
    Neglect of it does it no harm.

31.
Still, every day, the dawn
　　Brings a blessing
　　To whatever is growing
　　　　Towards the sun.

32.
I came to you only with hope in my mind.
I left you leaving my love behind.

33.
'Come to me here!'
　　Sings the evening star.
When the lamp's flames fail
　　They obey that call.

34.
　　In the joy of its flight
　　The bird seems to write
Letterless words in the sky.
　　When my flying mind sings
　　My pen is borne high
　　On the same joyous wings.

35.
'Hear us, hear us!' they cry,
　　Trading word for word.
Speech-merchants in droves
　　Struggle to be heard.

If your soul has something to say
    Deep within,
Keep it silently covered
    In the midst of that din.

36.
Watch the sculptor hone
An image from hard stone.
May life's restrictive frame
    Give form to non-form.

37.
Lotus in the fathomless lake —
    Who can gather it?
Grass growing under our feet —
    All are served by it.

38.
Tumultuous days
    Rush towards night.
Seas are the goal
    Of streams in full spate.
Impatient spring-flowers
    Long to be fruit.
Restlessness strives
    To be calm and complete.

39.
'I'll light a light,' said the star.
'Whether, if I do, the darkness will go,
      I do not know.'

40.
Night, though near, can't be seen.
Moon, though far, is well known.

41.
The black cloud thinks when it covers the stars,
      'I've won.'
  But the stars will be there
    Quite unperturbed,
    After the cloud
      Has gone.

42.
What we'll get from other people,
  Who will give and what:
Days are wasted idly thinking
  All about that.
One day we will have to leave
  Everything we've got.
What will *we* give when we go?
  Think about that.

43.
We carefully gather
What's scattered all over,

Tie up the random
To give it a price.
In the end the string snaps,
The bundles lapse
To former disorder,
Dusty oblivion.
Their paltry value, alas,
   Doesn't last forever.

44.

   Dust pulls back
   Any fame that I make;
   But my songs are retained
In Saraswati's veena-playing hand.[5]

45.

The flower's beauty
   When its petals fall
Hides as honey
   In the fruit's soul.

46.

A shooting star this night
   Has suddenly
   Entered my heart
And released a tear-stream of melody.

---

5.   Saraswati is the Hindu goddess of learning and the arts. She plays
   a veena.

47.

This, the last hope
    Of my weary pen:
    That its words will slip
Into the silent ocean
        Of meditation.

48.

In its sudden spontaneous surging and roaring
    The stream recognises itself.
In my own astonished surges of feeling
        I find my essential life.

49.

Yesterday's futile striving —
    Its dust and dirt —
Is washed away each morning
    By new hope's light.

50.

Trees in a shroud,
Hills in obscurity:
In the mist and cloud
What is this sorcery?
I listen to the stream's
Invisible murmur:
Its anxiousness seems
Like God's own whisper.

51.
The tree doesn't give fruit
    To pay a debt:
    Its whole life is giving.
If somebody comes to pick,
    The fruit is his luck —
    Not what is owing.

52.
The leaves in the trees,
In the spring and the rains,
    Tell a tale
Of which nothing remains
    When they fall
To blend with the soil.

53.
Let the mist be gone
From the mountains this morning,
Let a fresh dawn sun
Bring a new awakening.
Let silence be broken
By the message that comes
Flowing from heaven
In hundreds of streams.

54.
From afar it was so forbidding:
Such hard, high, merciless stone.

But now, having toiled the distance,
I find my misgivings have gone.
In the sky such warm invitation,
Such kind embrace in the air:
> In an alien land
> I seem to have found
> Familar kinship here.

55.
Music is made
From blocks in the road,
Frustration, confusion,
> Stop, start.
The rhythm of sadness
Creates transcendent delightfulness
> Through musical art.

56.
Anklets heard in the wood:
The *Wanderlust* in their jingle
Makes me want to travel.

57.
Material form disappears,
Created by body and effort.
Illusory form endures
Created by shadow and light.

58.

If you want to see truly
        What is bad
See it in the light of the good:
        Don't look blindly.

59.

Although I was not remiss
        At planting-time,
I let the right moment pass
        When harvest came.

60.

You keep on trying
To hide yourself away —
But your mind won't obey:
        Out it flies,
Whenever you open your eyes.

61.

Raga Vasant-Bahar[6]
On Chaitra's sitar:[7]
Its waves rise
        On the breeze.

---

6.   A compound raga, formed from a combination of the night raga
     Bahar with spring raga Vasant (which is also performed at night).
7.   Chaitra (*Caitra*) is the last month of the Bengali year: mid-March
     to mid-April.

62.

Birthdays keep coming
To remind us that life is renewed
Again and again
Like the day's bright happy return
Each morning.

63.

Taking in its hands
The Flute of the Known,
The Unknown plays
Its manifold sounds.

64.

Your guardian deity
Quietly grows
In your heart, mind and body
Its own *pūjā*-flowers.[8]
That your nights and days
May be filled with the beauty
And fragrance of these —
I bless your family.

65.

Ignoring fatigue,
O young traveller,

---

8. In Hindu worship or ritual (*pūjā*), it is customary to offer flowers
to a deity.

Journey staunchly
Down life's road.
May the travelling lamp that you carry
In your own heart
Burn inextinguishably.

66.
Life's puzzle
Sinks into death's conundrum.
Daylight's babble
Settles into starlight's calm.

67.
Into your life
New beauty has dawned:
May its dew-washed peace
Protect you all round.
At your life's midday
Let its sweetness assume
A powerful form.
Let it drive away
All weariness
From active goodness.

68.
In your life's lamp
May light's blessing
Rouse in the ignorant dark
A bright awakening.

69.

Light new life's pure lamp:
Hold up to mortality's eyes
    A letter from heaven.
Create in the depths of the dark
    Light's garden.
Inject a song of immortality
Into confused cacophony.

70.

To dive, one just
    Dives down straight.
To cross, one must
    Know how to float.

71.

An ocean wave
    Stares at the sun:
Says, 'That doll —
    Give it to me, someone!'

72.

The far horizon
    Of the sky of your mind
By sorrow's cloud-crimson
    Is royally crowned.

73.

The sea wants to understand
The message, written in spray,

That the waves repeatedly write
And immediately wipe away.

74.
The night-long whispered words of the stars
Bloom next day as woodland flowers.

75.
      Springtime bird,
You give the woodland shade the gift of tongues.
    Sky wants to sing with your voice
        Its own songs.

76.
You are building a house:
    My foundations are crumbling.
You are spoiling for a fight:
    I'm finished with struggling.
You are tuning your sitar:
    I've stopped at the *sam.*[9]
The circle requires for completeness
    My ending and your beginning.

77.
You are just you:
    The debt I owe

---

9.   In a *tāla* or rhythmic cycle in Indian classical music, the *sam* is the
    first beat, to which the cycle keeps returning.

I repay with my love
    Each day anew.

78.

The goodness you show
To those who serve you;
The unconditional love
You attract towards you;
Their unimaginable energy,
Their tireless vitality,
    Is not theirs by right:
    It's a gift, from you.

79.

The meeting I wanted so badly
    Foundered when you came close.
I was waiting, your seat was ready:
    You came from a distant place,
    Set foot in the yard of my house —
But then, smiling harshly,
    You turned, sped away with the pace
    Of a boat in an offshore wind:
    No thought of where you might land.

80.

When I look you in the eye
    Your face seems
Like someone only visible to me
        In dreams.

81.

Those rainless clouds
Assembling in crowds
At the edge of the sky
    Write to say:
Let the world enjoy
A sky-high holiday today.

82.

That travelling cloud
    About to disappear
Writes only its shade
    As its name on the air.

83.

When daylight dims
    And deep shadows fall
I come to the pond
    With a pitcher to fill.
Where lotuses shine
    I stand and stare
At the watery gleam
    Of a single star.

It does not sink
    And it does not fade —
It does not move
    When the ripples slide.
It seems to engrave
    On Time's dark screen

My nights of waiting
    For the might-have-been.

From my life's vain lamp
    A streak of fire —
Gleaming in the night:
    It lingers there.

84.

Daytime: the hours cross over,
    Bearing their burden of work.
Sunset: the boat's magic cargo
    Is coloured by light and dark.

85.

Day and night without sleeping,
    Eternity watches and waits
For a visitor who lives in no place,
    Whom no one can name,
Who exists beyond all imagining.

86.

The two shores yearn,
And the sea between
Sings of their bottomless pain.

87.

No hope in this life
    Of avoiding care.

O heart, have the strength
    Your grief to bear.

88.
With grief's lamp flaming
Search your mind.
Perhaps you will suddenly find
    Treasure everlasting.

89.
Grief is like a monsoon night:
    No halt in the teeming rain.
Joy is like lightning's message:
    Smiling, then vanishing again.

90.
When a wind from across the sea
    Comes to this shore,
Red fire ignites the Spring
And sparks the Ashoka-tree[10]
        Into golden fire.

91.
In the sky, a slender new moon,
Cut like a precious stone.

---

10 An evergreen tree whose springtime clusters of flowers turn from
    orange to scarlet.

92.

Wanting to play with the earth,
    The young pole star
Strayed away from the path,
    Came to night's shore.
Morning went out to look —
    Took the star home.
Light's wealth must go back
    To the light it is from.

93.

The new year has come today
    In the dark of a storm.
It has brought no message of hope;
    It offers no balm.
Adverse fortune arrives
In the shape of hate and dread.
The moment we succumb to fear,
    It raises its head.
Today, for the life I've been given
    Let me pay in full:
Let courage at a time of peril
    Settle the bill.

94.

What is given unasked for brings
    A massive enough debt.
If all you asked to have was yours,
    How would you pay for that?

95.

In empty, indolent leisure
    No peace is found.
Only in truthful work
    Is peace attained.

96.

On a birthday, view
        The new
    Within the old
            Unfold.

97.

    When a new age dawns,
    Some ageing brains
Finely weigh up their choices:
    When to depart?
    Should they travel or not?
They endlessly dip their worries
Into bottomless wells of doubt.
But you, young friend, be bolder!
Plunge into mountainous danger
Like a torrent into the fray;
Let obstacles stir your valour;
Be not afraid to discover
Your unknown destined way.

98.

Novelty speedily vanishes:
    It does not last.

Newness is always present,
   Though ages have passed.
The more we drink of novelty
   The thirstier we are.
Newness is an ageless nectar
   That quenches desire.

99.

The lotus spreads out its petals
   To receive what the sun's rays write.
What happens to that fleeting message
   When the sun sets at night?

100.

We live in a limited world
   Enclosed by what is familiar.
An unseen world is close by,
   Vaster and stranger.
Messages between the two
   Speak in a shadowy metre.
The wail of a distant flute,
   The scent of a nameless flower.

101.

When the sun sets in the West,
Let Purabi sound in your ears —
   Raga of the East.[11]

---

11. Purabi is an evening raga in Indian classical music, but the name
    is also cognate with *pūrba* ('east').

102.

When a bird sings a song
It does not know that it worships
    The sun's dawning.
When a flower blooms in the wood
It does not know that it makes
    Its *pūjā*-offering.[12]

103.

In your rocks and your peaks,
    O Mountain-King,
You have written over time
Each morning and evening
    In unknown writing
The endless tale
    Of the earth's ageing.
On a single page
    Of that vast history,
With just one line
    Will you make an entry:
That under your peaks
    We few were happy,
That for two merry days
    We enjoyed a party?

104.

With the past's pen in my hand
I write my name on the future.

---

12. See fn.8, p.123.

Superimposed are the signatures
    Of later writers.
In Time's notebook the muddle
Of old and new combined:
    A ceaseless scribble.

105.
Buds
    Bring solace
        To the woods.

106.
First glimmer of light breaks through:
Dawn dresses the grass with dew.
    The object of this show of praise
    Dries it up with its thirsty rays.

107.
A sunflower:
    Earth's picture
        Of the rising sun.
        Not fully pleased,
        Picture erased,
    With a new sunflower
Earth tries again.

108.
Let the flowers that bloom in the morning
    Give forth a beautiful scent.

Let them be rewarded in the evening
    With fruits that are succulent.

109.
Love's original fire fills
    The sky with white-hot flame.
Descending to earth it separates out
    Into colour, dress and form.

110.
The joy of love in our lives
    But briefly stays.
The pain of love endures
    To the end of our days.

111.
Spring has come to my door,
    But I've no one at home.
My heart calls out to someone:
    I don't know whom.

112.
A flower is hiding somewhere:
    Its fragrance gives it away.
In dreams, a life is hidden
    That songs convey.

113.

The wind tears the flowers
     Wantonly:
    They are unthinkingly cast
      To the dust.

The one who gathers the flowers
    And makes of them a garland
Considers such abandoned treasure
    Good enough to wear
      In her hair.

Do not ask of my song,
    For whom did I write it?
    In the dust it sits
Waiting for the one who confers
    Value on it.

114.

Love writes its name
In a script made of flowers.
They fall, but come back again.
Ambition is engraved
In harsh letters of stone.
When they break, they do not return.

115.

The bud receives such favour
From the morning sun.

When — its heart brimming over —
    Will its fruit be born?

116.
'Answer me, answer me, wife!'
    The more the bird sings,
The more its own racket
    Drowns the answers
       The woodland brings.

117.
Great work bears
    Its own burden.
Great grief supplies
    Its own consolation.
Small tasks, small hurts, small troubles
    Crush the life-spirit
       To near-suffocation.

118.
How easy it is
To mock the sun:
The light by which it is caught
    Is its own.

119.
Rain on a monsoon night
    Knocks petals off the jasmine-creeper.
Their scent makes the watery breeze
       Kind and tender.

120.

In the monsoon, under a *siuli*-tree,[13]
    Sit ready for prayer.
Weave a garland of fallen blooms,
    And of this be sure:
Their petals will quickly fade
But their beauty will not depart:
    If you look you will find it
    Somewhere in your heart.

It will stay as if locked in a chest:
Opened, the scent is released
        Of times past.

121.

The torrential glory of the cloud
        Is over.
It emptily nervously peeps
        From the sky's border.

122.

The messengers of Spring
    Sometimes bring
    A sighing gust
Of a season that is past.

---

13. Night jasmine; its small white flowers blossom at night and drop
     by early morning.

123.
The magical words
Spring writes in the woods —
Let their spell come down
    Into my pen.

124.
When a storm gatecrashes
    Springtime's party,
The young leaves smile,
    Buds feel easy.
Only leaves that are older
    Feel under threat;
But the storm will release them!
    Why fear that?

125.
When the Spring breeze maddens the woods,
    The leaves quiver and sway.
Their dance is a tribute to Beauty:
    'We are blessed,' they say.

126.
Form is tethered to matter;
    Rhythm to energy;
        Meaning to personality.

127.
Too long I've wandered from place to place,
Seen mountains and seas at vast expense.

Why haven't I stepped two yards from my house,
Opened my eyes and gazed very close
At a drop of dew on a stalk of rice?

128.
The lotus is asked by the breeze,
        'What is your mystery?'
'I myself,' it replies,
        'Am the mystery within me.'

129.
As soon as the wind blows
        And the first petals scatter,
Know at once that the rose
        Won't last much longer.

130.
When the lamp is blown out by the wind
        And stars can be seen,
Then though it is dark we can trace
        The path's line.
When happiness comes to an end
        And pleasures cease,
Then sorrow reveals to the mind
        The power of Peace.

131.
We fetch from without
        Pleasure's ingredients.

We find in ourselves
    Joy's determinants.

132.
Outside, the weight of possessions:
        So-called wealth;
    Within, in the heart's fulfilment:
          Spiritual health.

133.
I have found what I sought from door to door,
Thinking I'd lost it again and again.
I shall blend it with my life within,
In my forms and conceits make it mine,
And scatter its nectar outside once more.

134.
This fading light
    At my day's end,
Does it in the East
    Awaken some mind?
Light years yonder,
    The creative pain
That maddens the Creator,
    Will my journey perhaps
End at its centre?
    Does the sunset's shine
        Hint at that future?

135

Why is the *mādhabī*-branch so restive?
　　Why do its buds quiver?
What rustling words, shrouded in green,
　　　Does it whisper?[14]

136.

The noise of wheels departing
　　Still reach my ear from afar;
But the tearing of the bonds connecting
　　Makes no sound anywhere.

137.

God has respect for rebellion;
More than for blind devotion.

138.

The sky will be spotlessly robed in light,
The earth will sparkle with dew.
Your veena, O white *sephālī*,[15]
　　Will ring out pure and true.

139.

Who is this poet
　　At the world's core —

---

14. The *mādhabī*-creeper has bunches of pink or sometimes light yellow
flowers, with a faint, very pleasant smell. It blooms from February
to September.
15. See fn.14, p.63.

So keen to rewrite
    The poem of a flower?
His anguished heart
    Rubs it out once more.
For the pain of his art
    He finds no cure.

140.

When the sky of the mind is bright with truth,
When love anoints the earth of the heart,
Then graciousness blooms on the tree of life
And flowers of tenderness yield their fruit.

141.

I try to select the Best
    By setting snares.
It somehow gives me the slip:
    I lose it unawares.
Then I give my own self as a gift,
    Hands humbly folded.
By the Best, of its own volition,
    I am selected.

142.

Beloved, the pain you would give me,
    Give it
        Freely;
But take my sad heart nonetheless:
    Don't drop it
        Idly.

The flowers that you casually picked,
    In the wood,
        Unthinking,
Why do you leave them in the dust,
    So fast
        Forgetting?
Make them your garland,
        Rather:
Pierce them,
        String them
            Together.

143.

In the temple you serve, O votary,
If you don't want your worship to stop,
    Then show no inhumanity.
Love for all men is the only
Proof you can give of the love
    You feel for the temple's deity.

144.

The floating flower
    Cannot be caught:
That wave that would catch it
        Pushes it.

145.

My works are toys
    For Shiva to play with.

What suits him in the mornings
    By afternoon is finished with.[16]

146.
In the sky of the mind,
    Along its horizon,
The world-weary dream-bird
        Hastens on.

147.
Dust has returned to dust.
That which will last —
The heart's possession —
Remains in love's heaven.

148.
Stand indifferent to praise or censure,
Walk upon thorns without a murmur,
Scoop from the dust a tattered banner.
    Take from Destruction your final blessing,
    Learn that joy is a friend to grieving,
    Lose yourself in endless self-giving.

149.
You can't still be calling me,
You can't still be wanting me —

---

16. Because the great god Shiva destroys the universe so that it can be created afresh.

Old heart says.
Days of festival are over,
Oil-lamp is growing weaker,
   Last music plays.
I've paid off my rent now,
Settled all my debts now —
   Reached my final days.
I've songs and light enough to last me,
Got the gifts the world can give me,
No point in trying to call me —
   Last music plays.[17]

150.

Why, at our meeting
   (So happy a time)
Do your eyes with tears
   Fill to the brim?
And why on departing
   (Such heart's distress)
Do I see now
   A smile on your face?

151.

The flower must serve in the bud
   A dark imprisonment.

---

17. Literally, the music of *bisarjan*, the 'sacrifice' or immersion of the idol of Durga at the end of *Durgā-pūjā*, Bengal's main Hindu festival.

Beauty is happy to bear
  Such self-confinement.

152.
Up to the sky
My free thoughts roam:
In my songs they come home.

153.
Time doesn't stick:
  Yet still I dream
Of making my mark
  On ages to come.

154.
Earth by her nourishment binds the tree.
Sky by its light keeps setting it free.

155.
A life that must show its worth
      Through dying .
Is a life that will conquer Death
    Through Life Everlasting.

156.
When, under dawning skies,
Darkness opens its doors,
The golden music of sunrise
    Gathers the stars.

157.

When I hurried on down the road,
    My mind was set on the future —
I thought there was nothing close:
    What I wanted was many miles further:
Obsessed with reaching my goal,
    I pressed on forward grimly —
But now at the end of the road
    I turn and look behind me:
I see that along the verge
    What I wanted was already there:
What seemed so enticing ahead,
    Behind, can't be had any more.

158.

The grandest rainbow's a far-off thing.
I prefer what my patch of earth can bring:
The colours that paint a butterfly's wing.

159.

Gathering all that can be got,
    The game of life goes on:
But in Time's destructive dancing game
            It'll all be gone.

160.

All that I keep for myself,
    Serves no purpose.
Since I won't last, it too

Will be utterly useless.
What I keep instead for you all
   Only that will last:
It won't go under with me:
   You'll hold it fast.

161.

Don't you know that this single road
   Is a cul-de-sac?
If you block the journey ahead
   There's no way back.

162.

Rain, wind, sun through the years:
   A mountain-crag will dwindle;
Yet grass that so continually fades
     Has Life Eternal.

163.

Someone too blind to see his brother
Can't see his own self either.

164.

Those who in piety's name
   Store up hate,
Steal from the gifts to God
   On the *pūjā*-plate.

165.

On the branch where its bud was born
The flower that is not yet grown
Is blessed each day by the sun.

166.

You cannot call back
    One who goes.
Let memory burgeon —
    Watered by tears.

167.

The jewel that is best
    Cannot be traced
        If you search for it straight.
No one quite knows
    How it makes itself ours.
        When the time is right.

168.

Night becomes day:
    Birds, wake up,
Follow light's path
    To heaven's cup.

169.

Rain in the night runs riot
    In the *tamāl*-branches.[18]

_____

18. Tree with dark-green leaves and blackish bark and timber.

It drums at the nests of birds:
   'Wake up, wake up,' it urges.

170.
This world is made up
   Of forms and the formless.
Feelings give it music,
   Truth, the *logos.*
Come to the centre
   Of its sounds and pictures,
To the place in your mind
   Where Eternity whispers.

171.
I want, by working in the world,
   To bring to the fore
   The One who is hidden
   In my life's core.

172.
Though full of the damp air of autumn,
The clouds do not shed their rain.
Why do they hold back their feelings,
Stare with such stoical pain?

173.
The root decides, 'I'm sound.
   Branches have nothing there.
I stand firm in the ground.
   They live in empty air!'

174.

With nothing in his bag,
   The beggar wanders in vain.
But if he gives of himself,
   He receives from everyone.

175.

Behind the blank page
   There's a message lurking.
How can I call it
   Out of hiding?
If I give it no thought
   I find it in my heart.
If I call it direct
   It leaps back straight
      To its veiling.

176.

On the last night of spring
   I drained youth's sap
      From the cup of my painful longing.

177.

Black shade of Shraban
Falls on the *tamāl*-trees
   Like liquid collyrium
From a sky-goddess's eyes.[19]

---

19. Shraban (*Śrābaṇ*) is the second of the two monsoon months, mid-July to mid-August. For *tamāl* see previous note (p.151).

178.

In the green *bakul*-grove[20]
    Where the shade is complete,
A gentle tune seems to play
    To my footstep's beat.

179.

When the fierce pain of the world
    Deals us a blow,
'I am not here' are the words
    The heart seems to know.
He who is of all time
    Is detached from this era:
His body displays no sign
    Of the wounds we suffer.

180.

The name that is signed by the sun
On the clouds at the end of the day
Is erased when the clouds move away.

181.

    When we win success
    And bow our heads humbly,
We recognise all that remains
    Beyond our capacity.

---

20. See fn.3, p.41.

182.

He who loves above all
    The god of armament
Is himself destroyed, the more
    Those arms are triumphant.

183.

The time is approaching
    For me to depart,
    So I place my heart
In this youthful sapling.
    In the flowers and the green
Of its fresh leaves dancing,
    In the joy of spring coming
        My hopes will remain
        When I am gone.

184.

As the night goes by
    The stars blaze,
But on the smooth sky
    No mark stays.

185.

He who is lured by hedonism
    Is spurned by Delight.
Only the strings of heroism
    Tune Ecstasy's veena right.

186.

    A lotus as in our own land,
Smiling with the same sweet beauty,
Is blooming with another name, my friend,
    Far off, in another country.

187.

A sitar playing
Dhanshi raga:[21]
Exquisite melodic embellishments:
As though it is bringing
A woman nearer
In sunset-coloured habiliments.

188.

Brother kills brother when a war
    Is against God's law.

189.

Mixing crimson with gold,
Who has enmeshed the dreams
Of the roving sun with such colour?
When crossing darkness's river,
    If the colours fade,
At daybreak they all come back.
Sunset to sunrise coursing,

---

21. Probably Dhanashri, an afternoon raga, light, romantic and cheerful
in mood.

On its paths of going and coming,
The sun's own light pours down:
Receiving in cloud-corners,
In springtime trumpet-flowers,
Trays of colours in return.

190.

The motionless verge, unaware, unawake,
Stamped on by time, sinks into dust.
A river that tires on the way to the sea
Stagnates, weighed down by mud.
The lifeless light of a guttering lamp,
Hidden in the nook of a sleeping house,
    Fades before night is over.
A blazing light in a wayfarer's heart
Stays awake through the night,
Doesn't know how to mix with the dark.

191.

When cool clouds soothe
    The fierce hot sky,
It has no means
    To thank them by.
When parched hot earth
    Is cooled by showers,
It shows its thanks
    With fruits and flowers.

192.
Fanatical worship of memory,
Sacrificing the present
To praise what belongs to history!

193.
Venus, with her smile so bright,
Writes at day's dawning
A song of the coming of light
At darkness's ending.

194.
That which through nights and days
Has been sunk in Himalayan stillness,
Under seven star-sages' gaze,
Wrapped in speechless whiteness —
The melting of that ice-cascade
By the warmth of the sun's brightness
Releases on every side
A song of unending gladness!

195.
O dawn, come silently,
    Draw back the sky's
        Dark veil.
O life-force, inwardly
    Free what the buds
        Conceal.
O consciousness, wake,

Shake off the sleep
    Of dumb inertia.
O soul, roll back
    The dull dark drape
        Of prejudiced dogma.

196.

O tree, when I am no longer
    In the world,
May the passing wayfarer
    Be told
By the new leaves' murmur
    In Spring:
'The poet was a lover,
    Life-long.'[22]

197.

When, O my love, you appear,
In my thoughts, in Sorrow's guise,
It is then that I recognise:
    Joy is who you are.

198.

    I scatter carelessly
Words on the dusty ground,
    Which footsteps pound
    To dust very quickly.

---

22. See Introduction, p.22.

Appendix A

1. The following essay on *Lekhan* was first published in the Kārtik 1335 (October-November 1928) issue of *Prabāsī*, and reprinted by Visva-Bharati at the end of Volume 14 of the *Rabīndra-racanābalī*.

When I went to China and Japan, almost every day I had to satisfy the claims of autograph-hunters. I had to write for them often, on paper or silk or on fans. They wanted me to write in Bengali, because a signature in Bengali was on the one hand mine, on the other hand the whole Bengali nation's. I became in this way accustomed to writing two or four line poems at odd moments and wherever I happened to be; and I got pleasure from them. The concise expression achieved by concentrating one feeling[1] or another into a few lines has often given me more satisfaction than my longer compositions. I believe that because we have become

---

1.   *bhāba*. See Introduction p.22f.

used to reading longer poems we are reluctant to think of very short poems as real poems. Those who are used to overeating do not feel fully satisfied unless every corner of their stomach is loaded; the excellence of a meal is reduced for them if the quantity is limited. In our country there are many readers for whom size is what matters most: the bigger the book the better,[2] and tickets for a play are only worth buying if it lasts until three in the morning.

Among the Japanese, small poems are not at all despised. They like to see the big in the small, because they are born artists. They refuse to judge beauty by size or weight. So when anyone in Japan has asked me for a poem, I have had no compunction about giving them only two or four lines. When some years ago I wrote *Gitanjali* and other similar songs, many in Bengal counted the lines and were disappointed at my niggardliness: there is still no lack of such people.

When my pen started to flow with little poems of this sort, then even if no one asked me I seized my notebook and wrote whatever I fancied; and I humbly tried to placate my readers by saying:

My jottings are brief
    As a roadside flower
That passers-by see
    But do not remember.[3]

---

2. A Sanskrit tag is used here: *nālpe sukham asti* — 'Small isn't beautiful.'
3. *Lekhan* 2.

But then I came to see that this is not the fault of the fleeting flower, but of those who walk past. We tend not to stop and look at things that are small and unglamorous, but if we did, there would be no shame in being delighted by even the humblest flowering weed. It might be no less beautiful than a great big pumpkin flower.

When I went to Italy last time, I had to write a lot in autograph-books. Those who wanted me to write often asked for it to be in English. At this time too, sometimes in their notebooks and sometimes in mine, lots of little poems of this sort accumulated. The writing often begins in this way — on request — but then the urge takes over and I don't need to be asked.

When I went to Germany I found out that a way had been invented of printing directly from handwriting. One has to write with special ink on a sheet of aluminium, and by printing from that with a special machine one can avoid the tender mercies of the compositor altogether.

Then I wondered if those who did not regard tiny poems as literature would perhaps accept them in the poet's own handwriting. I was rather unwell at the time, and therefore had plenty of time on my hands; so I got on with writing these little English and Bengali poems on to aluminium sheets.

Meanwhile a young friend of mine happened to say, 'You have quite a few small poems from some time back. It would be excellent if you could use this opportunity to preserve them.'

I'm extremely good at forgetting things, and I often develop an inexplicable aversion to my earlier writings. So when the younger generation of writers starts plotting to strip me of my literary name, my better judgement tells me, 'Why not give up beforehand, write a resignation-letter myself and put in a claim for a small pension?' I can think in this way, because the more forgetful I become of my early writings the more I assume that they deserve to be forgotten.

I was therefore all prepared, if my friend brought me his gleanings from the field of ancient history, to send them straight back acoss the *Vaitaraṇi* [4] to the dark world of the past.

He turned up with only about five small poems. I said, 'I shan't be able to remember at all if these are my poems.' 'They are certainly yours,' he insisted.

My own testimony with regard to my compositions is always untrustworthy. My songs, for example: I'm always thinking up tunes for them. I sing the tunes to whoever happens to be at hand. Thereafter, responsibility for the tunes rests entirely with my pupils. If later I try to sing them, they are quite ready to say that I've got them wrong. I frequently have to accept correction from them in this.

I accepted that the handful of poems my friend showed me were mine. I was rather pleased when I read them: they seemed to me quite well written. If, through my immense capacity for forgetfulness, my mind becomes distant from my own poems, I am able to admire them or criticise them with detachment, like any other reader. Because the edge of my vanity about them has been blunted, I am not shy about feeling or admitting that I am impressed by them. I had a look at this one:

> The fact that my thoughts are always centred on you
> Won't cause anyone else in this world any hurt.

---

4. River in the Hindu underworld: equivalent to the Styx.

It won't impoverish me, and you won't be in my debt;
    Even God will get his rightful due.

Even though I thought this poem was my own, I had to admit that it said a great deal in a little. To satisfy the stomach of a gluttonous reader, it could have been expanded to twenty-five or thirty lines: it might even have been easier to make it longer. But a greedy increase in size would only have reduced its effect. So I praised it with my own ungreedy sensibility.

Next, this one:

Since dawn, the blue sky has been covered with black cloud:
    A damp wind blows chaotically, gust after gust.
    Feelings have drained away, alas, from my breast.
    The wind and sky have taken over my mood.

'Well done,' I said to myself again. The sky and the howling wind filling the heart's emptiness — who in Bengali literature has said this so easily and so completely? There's no way one can add a single word. I congratulated myself on restraining my pen, even though I knew that the myopic reader would not be able to see beauty in so small a poem.

Then another:

Thick cloud, deep rumbling in the sky:
The world is flooded with Shraban torrents.[5]
How can you so flippantly call me
By my nickname? Today is a day
For full names: it's not a time

---

5.   See fn.19, p.153

For amorous banter and frivolity.
Earth and sky are dark and trackless:
The day of ultimate reckoning has arrived.

This belongs to my *Mānasī* phase:[6] it's not what I would write today. I remember writing one or two poems like this. But through some kind of divine power of reduction,[7] the mood has been expressed in an extremely slender form.

One more short poem:

If on my life's road, Lord,
I keep on taking
The weight you have given me
Down from my head,
Know this is not
Rebelliousness,
But just my frail weary heart,
My feebleness of spirit.

Because the poem is so utterly unadorned, its inner suffering blooms like a jasmine-flower battered by the rain.

With great satisfaction and pride, I copied these few poems in my own hand on to aluminium sheets. In due course these poems along with other brief poems of mine[8] were published in the book called *Lekhan*.

6.　Tagore's collection of poems, *Mānasī* was published in 1890.

7.　*Aṇimāsiddhi:* the power by which supernatural beings can turn themselves into wraiths and move everywhere almost invisibly. 'Mood' here is *bhāba.*

8.　The coinage *kabitikā* ('poemlet') is used. See Introduction, p. 3.

A few months ago I sent a copy of *Lekhan* to the gracious Srimati Priyambada Devi.[9] I quote here the letter that she wrote in reply:

I have read *Lekhan*. Some of the little poems in it are excellent: complete in two or three lines — but each poem is like a finely-cut, sparkling gem. On p.23 of *Lekhan* I've noticed four whole poems of my own, and one whose first two lines are by me. They are:

1. 'The fact that my thoughts are always centred on you'
2. 'Since dawn, the blue sky has been covered with black cloud'
3. 'Thick cloud, deep rumbling in the sky'
4. 'If on my life's road, Lord'
5. 'Only this little happiness, so tender' (first two lines)

They were all published in my book *Patralekhā* in 1908. But please don't say anything about this to anyone else.

I then remembered that when I read the manuscript of *Patralekhā* I had given high praise to Priyambada's spare and unornamented poems. Probably their spareness was the reason why they did not receive the recognition they deserved. I am happy, at least, that I expressed my admiration for her poems by erroneously giving these few poems in *Patralekhā* a place in my own book in my own handwriting!

---

9.   See Introduction, p.12.

2. The following extract is from Chapter 13 of *Jāpān-yātrī* ('Traveller to Japan', 1919), which collected together Tagore's various letters and writings about his visits to Japan in 1916 and 1917. (See Introduction, p.10.) The book is included in Volume 19 of *Rabīndra-racanābalī*, pp.338-340.

One thing particularly strikes me about public places in Japan. There are crowds of people in the streets, but no noise. It's as if they don't know how to shout; people say that even children in Japan do not wail. So far, I haven't seen a single child crying. When driving along, if a car gets held up by hand-carts etc., the driver simply waits quietly — he doesn't curse, he doesn't yell out. In our country, if a bicycle suddenly got in the way of a car, the driver would not be able to resist hurling unnecessary abuse. Our Japanese driver never bats an eyelid. The Bengalis here have told me that if there is a collision between a bicycle and a car, or between two bicycles, and the riders suffer cuts and scratches, they just dust themselves down and continue on their way, without shouting or cursing at all.

I think this must be the root cause of Japan's power. The Japanese do not waste their energy on pointless shouting and quarrelling. Because there is no unnecessary expense of energy, they have no lack of it when it is really needed. This physical and mental calm and patience forms a vital part of their national character. In grief, sorrow, pain or excitement, they know how to control themselves. That's why foreigners often say that the Japanese cannot be understood: they are inscrutable. The reason for this is that they do not let themselves spill out through cracks or holes in their self-control.

This extreme economy of self-expression can also be seen in their poetry. Nowhere else in the world does one find poems of only three lines. These three lines are enough for both poets and readers. That is why, since arriving here, I've heard no one singing in the street. Their hearts are not like a noisy gushing fountain, but are as still as the waters of a lake. All the poems that I have so far heard are pictorial; they are not poems that can be sung. People rarely let their energy be dissipated by fire or pain in the heart. Their inner feelings find expression in their appreciation of beauty. The appreciation of beauty is not a self-centred thing. Flowers, birds, the moon — our cries and moans are not caused by them. Our relationship with them stems purely from our sense of beauty — they do not buffet us, or snatch at us; they do not cause any destruction in our lives. Therefore three lines are sufficient for them; they do not disturb us even in our imagination.

If you take these two famous old Japanese poems as an example, my point will be clear:

An old pond,
>   The jump of a frog,
>   A splash of water.[10]

That's all! No need for any more. The Japanese reader's mind sees only images. The old pond is deserted by human beings, motionless, dark. As soon as a frog jumps into it, there is a splash. The noise

---

10. This is a literal rendering of Tagore's Bengali version. See Nobuyuki Yuasa's essay, 'Translating "The Sound of Water": different versions of a *hokku* by Bashō', in *The Translator's Art: essays in honour of Betty Radice*, edited by William Radice and Barbara Reynolds (Penguin, 1987), pp. 231-240.

of the splash shows how still the pond is. The poet only hints at how the old pond should be pictured in the mind; more than that is unnecessary.

Here's the other poem:

> A rotten branch,
>> A crow,
>>> Autumn.

Nothing more than that! In autumn there are no leaves on the tree-branches, one or two branches have rotted, a crow is perching on one of them. In a cold country, autumn is the season when leaves are shed, flowers fall, the sky is pale with mist: the season brings thoughts of death. A black crow is sitting on a rotten branch: from this the reader gets a complete mental picture of the emptiness and paleness of autumn. The poet simply starts the picture, and then stands aside. The reason why he has to withdraw so quickly, is that the Japanese reader has a remarkable capacity for visualising appearances.

I now give an example of a poem that has more to it than meets the eye:

> Heaven and earth are flowers,
>> The gods and Buddha are flowers —
>>> The human heart is the soul of a flower.

I feel that in this poem there is an affinity between Japan and India. Japan takes heaven and earth to be as beautiful as flowers in bloom; India says, there are two flowers on one stem, heaven and earth, God and Buddha. If there were no human heart, then these flowers would merely be external things: the essence of their beauty is in the human heart.

Anyway, in these poems there is not just restraint in the words, but restraint in the feeling too.[11] The stirrings of the heart nowhere disturb this restraint of feeling. I believe that this is profoundly characteristic of Japan. In sum, one might call it 'economy of heart'.

3. A short extract from Nirmalkumari Mahalanobis's memoir of her travels with Tagore, *Kabir sange yūrope* ('To Europe with the Poet', Calcutta, 1969), pp.255-6. See Introduction, p.12.

When we were in Berlin that time, Prasanta Babu[12] said to the poet: 'A brand new kind of printing machine has come on to the market — an excellent thing. It's very small; there are thin aluminium sheets, the size of foolscap paper. One has to write on those by hand, and one's handwriting can simply be printed straight from them. It isn't very big or heavy: you can easily take one home with you if you want.'

The poet was always very keen to try out anything new. He immediately gave the order: 'Buy the machine tomorrow.'

The next day the 'Rotar Print' machine arrived, with a sheaf of aluminium sheets to write on. My job was to sit and rule pencil lines on these thin sheets, to stop the poet's lines from going crooked.

Whenever Rabindranath had time, he would write little poems to print on the Rotar Print machine. He was delighted that his dependence on the printing-press would be considerably reduced. It was thanks to the Rotar Print that the whole of the book *Lekhan* came out in Rabindranath's own handwriting.

---

11. *bhāba* is used again here.
12. Her husband, Prasanta Chandra Mahalanobis.

This is among the many incidental images that have stayed in my mind: the poet writing away happily, while I sat next to him ruling lines on the blank aluminium sheets. Many people probably do not know why it was that the whole of *Lekhan* was published in Rabindranath's handwriting, even though he mentioned in his preface that he had it printed in handwriting after hearing about this machine in Germany. At first he thought he would call the book *Sphuliṅga*. Then he changed his mind and called it *Lekhan*.

Appendix B

Tagore's essay *Ādhunik kābya* ('Modern Poetry') first appeared
in the journal *Paricay* in Baiśākh 1339 (April-May 1932). It was
later included in the volume *Sāhityer pathe* ('On Literature's
road', 1936). The quotations from English and Chinese poetry
were nearly all taken from *The New Poetry: an anthology of
twentieth-century verse in English*, edited by Harriet Monroe
and Alice Corbin Henderson (New York: The Macmillan
Company, 1917; rev. 1923, 1932) and *The Works of Li Po the
Chinese Poet*, translated by Shigeyoshi Obata (New York: E. P.
Dutton & Co., 1922). They are mostly translated into Bengali
in the essay, but I have restored the English texts. Most of them
are mentioned in the Notes at the end of Visva-Bharati's edition
of *Sāhityer pathe*.

    The New Poetry included poems by Tagore himself: six from
Gitanjali (1912) and nine from *The Gardener* (1913). The six
poems from *Gitanjali* (Nos. 63, 89, 20, 32, 95 and 67) had earlier
been published in December 1912 in *Poetry*, the journal that

Harriet Monroe founded in Chicago in October of that year. They appeared just before the India Society in London published its complete edition.

I have been asked to write something about modern English poets. It's not an easy task, for who can determine the limits of the modern by the calendar? It's a matter not so much of time as of feeling.[1]

A river may follow a straight course, then suddenly turn a corner. Literature, too, does not always follow a straight line. When it suddenly turns, the twist in its course has to be called modern. In Bengali the word is *ādhunik*. This modernity is not dictated by time, but by temperament.

The English poetry that I knew in my childhood could be counted as modern then. Poetry had taken a new turn, beginning with the poet Burns. A number of great poets were associated with this trend: Wordsworth, Coleridge, Shelley, Keats.

In a society, the pattern of behaviour followed by the majority of people is known as 'custom'. In some countries, custom completely suppresses independence and variety of personal taste. People become puppets: their movements are rigidly controlled by etiquette. A high value is placed on these traditional norms. Sometimes literature too is controlled by lengthy tradition — writing that follows the rules precisely is regarded as correct. With Burns, an era in English poetry arrived in which the walls of convention were broken down in favour of individual taste. The 'lily-and-lotus-adorned-lake'[2] is a lake that is seen through ready-

---

1. *bhāba*. See Introduction, p.22f.
2. A Sanskrit poetic cliché is used here.

made slits in a standard-issue blindfold. When, by tearing off the blindfold and setting aside clichés, a brave new writer looks at the lake with unobstructed vision, he opens up a path that reveals the lake in various new moods and aspects. Correctitude cries 'Shame'.

When we began to read English poetry, literature had accepted this convention-breaking spirit of individuality. The growling of the *Edinburgh Review* had by then died down. A turning point had been passed in the development of modernity.

In those days, to be modern was to run with one's personal feelings. Wordsworth expressed in his own style the joyous spirit that he felt in Nature. Shelley was stirred by Platonism, together with rebellion against all kinds of political and religious oppression. Keats' poetry stemmed from the contemplation and creation of formal beauty. During that era, the stream of poetry turned from the external to the internal.

If a feeling lies deep in a poet's consciousness, it wants to give permanent form to itself through beauty of linguistic expression. Love adorns itself: it wants, through beauty, to prove externally the joy it carries within. In the era that came, man stood back to look at his immediate world and find ways of decorating it. This exterior decoration was an expression of inner affection. Where there is affection, there cannot be indifference. People at that time took delight in putting their personal stamp on objects of daily use. Inner desire gave creative skill to their fingers. All over the land, utensils, furnishings and clothes captivated human hearts with their beautiful appearance. People created all sorts of entertainments, to add richness to their lives. New kinds of music; new kinds of craft, using wood, metal, porcelain, stone, silk, wool, cotton. It was the desire of husbands that their wives should be their beloved followers, 'accomplished in the fine arts'.[3] For a couple wanting to set up a home together, money in the bank was not of primary concern; more important was the cultivation of the arts. It was no longer enough to throw a garland together; young ladies learned to paint on Chinese silk, to excel at dancing, play musical instruments, sing. In human relationships, the meeting of souls became all important.

The English poets we knew in my youth were connecting the outside world to their feelings: they made it individually their own. Their mentalities, opinions and tastes did not simply make the world human and psychological: each poet conceived it differently. Wordsworth's world was specifically Wordsworthian; Shelley's was Shelleyan; Byron's was Byronic. Through the magic of their writing, it became the reader's possession too. What pleased us about a particular poet's world was its special hospitality. Flowers invite bees with the special character of their colour and scent, and that letter of invitation is enchanting. There was a natural charm, too, in these poets' invitations. In eras when man's personal relationship with the world is dominant, one needs to ensure that an invitation has a personal touch: one competes, as it were, to make one's identity attractive through dress and ornament and grace.

Clearly, at the beginning of the nineteenth century, the priority shifted from the conventionality of the previous age towards self-expression. This was what was modern then.

But today, that kind of modernity has been termed old-

---

3.   A Sanskrit tag is used here.

fashioned mid-Victorianism, and has been relegated to a comfortable armchair in a side-room. Today, modernity lies in short-cut clothes and the severity of cropped hair. Not that powder is never applied to cheeks or lipstick to lips; but it is done brazenly, conspicuously, as if to say: 'There's no need any more for illusion.' Illusion is present in every step of God's Creation: varieties of illusion produce new tunes, new kinds of beauty. But science has analysed everything inside and out and established that there is no illusion at source: there is simply carbon and nitrogen and physiology and psychology. We are poets of the previous age; we discounted such realities; to us, the magic of illusion was primary. So we tried — I must admit — to compete with the Creator by engendering illusion through rhythm, form, language and style. Our hints and suggestions involved some deception; but decorum's coverings are not antagonistic to Truth, they are Truth's embellishments — we couldn't dispense with them. In the crimson glow that shines through decorum's misty haze, we saw the beauty of dawn or sunset — demure as a new bride. Modernity, like Duhshasana, has started to strip clothes off the universal Draupadi in public[4]: this is a sight that we are not used to. Is that why we feel embarrassed? If one discards the coverings that express rather than conceal, doesn't that impoverish Beauty?

But in the mind of the modern age there is impatience, hurry, a lack of time. Livelihood has become more important than Life.

---

4.   Draupadi is the wife of the five Pandava brothers in the *Mahābhārata*. When the eldest brother Yuddhisthira loses at dice to his cousins the Kauravas, Draupadi becomes their slave. Duhshasana, one of the Kauravas, starts to strip her clothes off, but the god Krishna replaces them as fast as they are torn off.

Swept along by a plethora of speed-inducing machines, we hurry both our work and our pleasures. The man who previously created his own world to suit himself, now sets it up in a purely utilitarian way, ordering whatever he needs from the factory as quickly as possible, to a uniform pattern. Pleasurable eating has gone; eating is all that remains. No thought is given to whether Life is in harmony with Mind, because Mind is set on pulling the rope of Livelihood's huge juggernaut, along with the crowd. Songs have been replaced by a perpetual 'Heave-ho, heave-ho'. More time is spent now in the public sphere, rather than the private. Mental activity has become perpetually rushed. In the general hurly-burly, no one is concerned to avoid the crude and ugly.

What route, therefore, should poetry take? What aim should it have? Choosing, arranging, decorating according to one's own taste won't do any more. Science doesn't choose; it has to take things as they are; it does not value things according to personal taste; it does not arrange things out of individual, affectionate interest. The chief joy of the scientific mind lies in curiosity, not in forming personal ties. What I myself might like is of no consequence to it: it considers what a thing actually is, by leaving me out of the picture. If I am left out, the construction of illusion is unnecessary.

Thus in the poetry of this scientific age, the greatest cuts in expenditure have been made to embellishment. It has gone for maximum economy of metre, form and language. This has not been done spontaneously; determined rejection of what entranced the previous age has become the norm. Its tactic — lest the power of choice should revert to its accustomed freedom, leap over the wall and enter the house — is to put ugly broken glass along the top of the wall. A poet has written: 'I am the greatest laugher of all'.[5] He says that he is a greater laugher than the sun, the oak tree, the frog or the god Apollo. 'Than the frog and Apollo': that's

---

5.   Tagore is quoting from the end of 'No prey am I', the third and last part of *Songs of Deliverance* by Orrick Johns (1887-1946), a Whitmanesque, 7-page sequence that was first published in *Poetry* in February 1914. In the Notes to the third edition of *The New Poetry* in 1932, it is described as 'a flare-up of youth's rebellion against the preceding generation.' It concludes:

> How often I have intercepted thee, O Death!
> O windy Liar!
> Thou canst do nothing against me;
> If I command thee to stand back thou art afraid and cowerest,
> For I have caught thee often and punished thee...
>
> I am the greatest laugher of all,
> Greater than the sun and the oak-tree,
> Than the frog and Apollo;
> I laugh all day long!
> I laugh at Death, I hail Death, I kiss her on the cheek as a lover his bride,
> But the lover goes not to his bride unless he desire her;
> I go not to Death until I am ready.
> The strong lover goes not to his bride save when he would people his land with sons,
> Then I too, I go not to Death, save it be for the labor greater than all others.
> I shall break her with my laughter;
> I shall complete her...
> Only then shall Death be when I die!

The death-imagery here is quite reminiscent of Tagore's *Gitanjali*, though the mood is different.

the broken glass — lest anyone think that the poet has smoothed anything over. If he had said 'the ocean' instead of 'the frog', the present age might have reviled it as a poetic cliché. Maybe; but in an opposite way, the frog is even more of a cliché. It's there to say: this has not been written naively, but in order to push and trample. This is a trick of the modernist's trade.

Certainly, the days when a frog was inappropriate in polite poetry are now over. In the House of Truth, a frog is not bigger or smaller than Apollo. I too do not wish to ignore frogs. I would even not be averse to mentioning the frog's croaking laugh in the same line as the laugh of a Beloved — whatever her objection. But even by the strictest laws of scientific impartiality, the laugh that is the sun's, the laugh that is the oak's, the laugh that is Apollo's, is not the laugh of a frog. He has been forcibly brought into the line in order to dispel illusion.

By stripping away all illusion, things must be seen as they are. That which in the nineteenth century was coloured by enchantment has today become drab; hunger can no longer be satisfied by a mere hint of sweetness; it wants something substantial. To say that 'smelt is half-eaten' would now be a gross exaggeration.[6] Here is what a modern woman poet has said in the clearest language about a beautiful woman of the last century:[7]

> You are beautiful and faded
> Like an old opera tune

---

6. A proverbial Sanskrit phrase is used here.
7. Tagore says about his Bengali translation here: 'It would not be appropriate to add any lyrical embellishment, and there'd be no point in trying either.'

Played upon a harpsichord;
Or like the sun-flooded silks
Of an eighteenth-century boudoir.
In your eyes
Smoulder the fallen roses of outlived minutes,
And the perfume of your soul
Is vague and suffusing,
With the pungence of sealed spice jars.
Your half-tones delight me,
And I grow mad with gazing
At your blent colors.

My vigor is a new-minted penny,
Which I cast at your feet.
Gather it up from the dust,
That its sparkle may amuse you.[8]

This kind of modern penny does not have much value, but it's tough and forthright: if you tap it, it rings with the music of the present age. The sweetness in the past age was intoxicating, but there was haughtiness in it too. The poem is absolutely frank about this.

The subjects of today's poetry do not aim to charm the mind with gracefulness. What therefore is its chief strength? Its strength is its energetic self-confidence, what in English is called 'character'. It says, '*Ayam aham bhoha!*' — 'Here I am!'[9] This same woman poet, whose name is Amy Lowell, has written a poem about a red

---

8. 'A Lady', by Amy Lowell (1874-1925); from *The New Poetry*.
9. Sanskrit again.

slipper-shop. It describes the icy blast of the evening wind outside the shop, and inside — behind the polished window-glass — long rows of red slippers hanging on strings

> ...like stalactites of blood, flooding the eyes of passers-by with dripping colour, jamming their crimson reflections against the windows of cabs and tram-cars, screaming their claret and salmon into the teeth of the sleet, plopping their little round maroon lights upon the tops of umbrellas.
>
> The row of white, sparkling shop fronts is gashed and bleeding, it bleeds red slippers....[10]

The whole of the poem is about these red slippers.

One can call it detached, 'impersonal'.[11] There's no particular reason to be attracted to this string of slippers, either for the customer or the shopkeeper. But one has to stand and look at it: there's some inner quality in the entire spectacle that suddenly gives it significance. Those who delve for meanings will ask, 'What are you getting at, sir? Why make such a fuss about slippers, even if they are red?' One can only reply, 'Just look.' 'What good will that do?' No answer to that.

There is a poem by Ezra Pound about aesthetics. It goes like this. A girl is walking along a street. A little boy, in patched clothes, suddenly catches sight of her. He can't restrain himself from calling out, 'Look, how beautiful!' Three years later, the poet sees the boy again. That year there has been a huge catch of

---

10. 'Red Slippers', from *The New Poetry*. Tagore quotes this passage in English.
11. The English word is used.

sardines. His uncles and brothers are arranging the fish in large wooden boxes, to send to the market at Brescia. The boy is larking about, mixing up the fish, disturbing their arrangement. His elders snap at him: 'Sit still.' He then runs his hand over the carefully laid out fish and in his pleasure murmurs to himself precisely the same words: 'Look, how beautiful!' The poet says, on hearing this, 'I was mildly abashed.'[12]

Don't be shy of using the same language, of saying 'Look, how beautiful!' about a girl or a sardine. This kind of looking is impersonal: sheer looking. The slipper-shop is observed in the same detached way.

Subjectivity was what counted in nineteenth century poetry; in twentieth century poetry, objectivity. The emphasis therefore now falls on the reality of a poem's subject-matter, rather than on rhetorial embellishment. This is because embellishment expresses personal taste; the strength of genuine realism lies in the subject's expression of itself.

Before its arrival in literature, this kind of modernism prevailed in painting. It began in various ways to deny the notion that painting was just a branch of the decorative arts. It said: Art's work is not to suspend the intellect, but to engage it; it is defined not by prettiness, but by veracity. In appearance, we no longer look for charm, but for 'character' — the expression

---

12. 'The Study in Aesthetics', from *The New Poetry*. In the original poem, the exclamations are in Italian: *Guarda! Ahi, guarda! ch'e be'a!...sta fermo...Ch'e be'a.* Also, the boy is one of a group of 'very small children in patched clothing' who call out at the girl; three years later, the poet recognises him, and hears him saying the same thing about the sardines.

of the self as a whole. Appearance does not want to say anything
about itself, other than to insist, 'I'm worth looking at.' It is
worth looking at not because of its pose, or its accurate copying
of nature, but because of its inner creative truth. This truth is
not religious or ethical or philosophical: it's creative. That is,
it has to be accepted simply because it has come into existence
— just as we accept the existence of a vulture no less than that
of a peacock; just as we cannot deny the existence of a pig, any
more than that of a deer.

Some things are beautiful, some are ugly; some are useful,
some are useless. But in the realm of creation under no pretext
can anything be left out. The same in literature as in painting. If
a genuine form has been created, there is no need to give any
further explanation; if it hasn't, if it has no convincing reality, if
it is there simply to charm the senses, then it should be discarded.

Thus the literature nowadays that espouses the gospel of
modernity dismisses the decorum of the previous age: the notion
that one must at all costs preserve caste by matching it. It is
indiscriminate. Eliot's poetry is of this sort; Bridges' is not. Eliot
has written:

> The winter evening settles down
> With smell of steaks in passageways.
> Six o'clock.
> The burnt-out ends of smoky days.
> And now a gusty shower wraps
> The grimy scraps
> Of withered leaves about your feet
> And newspapers from vacant lots;
> The showers beat

On broken blinds and chimney-pots,
And at the corner of the street
A lonely cab-horse steams and stamps.

And then the lighting of the lamps.

Then comes a description of a morning that is smeared with mud
and stinking with beer. On this morning, a girl is spoken of like
this:

You tossed a blanket from the bed,
You lay upon your back, and waited;
You dozed, and watched the night revealing
The thousand sordid images
Of which your soul was constituted....

Then a man is described:

His soul stretched tight across the skies
That fade behind a city block,
Or trampled by insistent feet
At four and five and six o'clock;
And short square fingers stuffing pipes,
And evening newspapers, and eyes
Assured of certain certainties,
The conscience of a blackened street
Impatient to assume the world.

On this utterly tawdry evening — smoky and grimy, full of stale
smells and tattered rubbish — and on this equally tawdry morning,
an entirely different kind of picture forms in the poet's mind.
He says:

I am moved by fancies that are curled
Around these images, and cling:
The notion of some infinitely gentle
Infinitely suffering thing....

Here the equivalence of Apollo and the frog breaks down.
Here the croaking sound of a frog in a well does an injury to
Apollo's smile. It is clearly apparent that the poet is not entirely
detached, as one would be in science. His distaste for the mundane
world shows through his description of it. That is why what he
says at the conclusion of the poem is so harsh:

Wipe your hand across your mouth, and laugh;
The worlds revolve like ancient women
Gathering fuel in vacant lots.[13]

The poet's aversion to this decrepit, fuel-gathering world can be
clearly seen. The difference between this and the previous era, is
that he has no desire to distract himself with a world formed from
his own colourful dreams. He wants to make poetry walk through
this muddy, murky world, without regard for its spotlessly laundered
clothes. Not because he has any liking for mud, but because, in
a muddy world, mud has to be acknowledged and accepted. If
Apollo's smile shines somewhere in the midst of this, that's good;
if it doesn't, even then there is no need to despise the frog's
jumping and guffawing. That also has validity; one can watch it

---

13. 'Preludes', from *Prufrock and Other Observations* (1917). Tagore
quotes the section 'His soul stretched tight...Infinitely suffering
thing' in English; the rest he translates into Bengali.

for a while as part of the universe; there's something to be said for it too. The frog would be out of place in the drawing-room of decorous language; but most of the world lies outside that drawing-room.

One wakes up in the morning. On waking up, the first thing is awareness of oneself: a new stirring of consciousness. One can call this state of mind romantic. The freshly awakened consciousness steps outside to test itself. The mind finds shapes for its thoughts and desires in Nature's creations, or creations of its own. It fashions external projections of what it wants within. Then the light grows sharper, experience becomes harsher, and the web of the mind's imaginings gets torn by the world's disturbances. In the clear light of day, under the naked sky, reality comes closer. Different poets pay homage to this familiar reality in different ways. Some look at it rebelliously, with cynical eyes; some are so disrespectful of it that they do not shrink from treating it cruelly and shamelessly. Then again there are some who feel a deep mystery even in what is clearly visible in the light of day: they do not think that there are no secrets, that nothing lies beyond what can be perceived by the senses. In the last European war, human experience was so barbaric and cruel; everything that had for generations been considered decent and civilised was suddenly shattered by so frightful a catastrophe, that the sure beliefs that had long given stability to society were immediately torn asunder. On seeing the destruction of everything they had esteemed as decorous and civilised, people began to take a kind of reckless delight in rejecting age-old politeness as weakness, as an artificial form of self-deception. Today, to hurl abuse at the world is regarded as deference to Truth.

But if modernism has an essential feature; if that feature can be given an impersonal definition; then it will have to be said that this kind of bumptious cynicism about the world, this abusive view of it, is itself a distortion of personal consciousness, born of a sudden shock. It too is obsessive: in it too, the easy acceptance of reality with calm objectivity is profoundly lacking. Many suppose that this severity, this iconoclastic battering, *is* modernism. I do not believe so. Just because influenza nowadays attacks thousands of people, I do not say that influenza is the body's modern nature. It's an external thing. Behind influenza lies the body's natural state.

If you were to ask me what pure, true modernism might be, I would say that it is a way of looking at the world with undistorted attentiveness, free of personal attachment. This vision is bright and pure; in this undeluded vision there is genuine joy. If modern poetry could look at the world whole, and with detachment, in the way that modern science analyses reality with detachment, then it would achieve everlasting modernity.

But then, to call it 'modern' would be utter nonsense! This kind of easy, detached joy in seeing does not belong to any particular time. It belongs to anyone whose eyes know how to rove through an uncovered world. The Chinese poet Li Po was writing more than a thousand years ago. He was modern: he looked at the world with fresh eyes. In four lines of simple language he wrote:

Why do I live among the green mountains?
I laugh and answer not, my soul is serene:
It dwells in another heaven and earth belonging to no man.
The peach trees are in flower, and the water flows on....[14]

---

14. 'In the Mountains', from *The Works of Li Po*, p.71. Tagore translates this and the following two poems complete: the dots are as in Obata's version.

Appendix B

Here's another picture —

> Blue water...a clear moon...
> In the moonlight the white herons are flying.
> Listen! Do you hear the girls who gather water-chestnuts?
> They are going home in the night, singing.[15]

And another —

> Naked I lie in the green forest of summer....
> Too lazy to wave my white feathered fan.
> I hang my cap on a crag,
> And bare my head to the wind that comes
> Blowing through the pine trees.[16]

And here's a young wife talking —

> I would play, plucking flowers by the gate;
> My hair scarcely covered my forehead, then.
> You would come, riding on your bamboo horse,
> And loiter about the bench with green plums for toys.
> So we both dwelt in Chang-kan town,
> We were two children, suspecting nothing.
>
> At fourteen I became your wife,
> And so bashful that I could never bare my face,
> But hung my head, and turned to the dark wall;
> You would call me a thousand times,
> But I could not look back even once.
>
> At fifteen I was able to compose my eyebrows,
> And beg you to love me till we were dust and ashes.

---

15. 'Nocturne', *ibid.*, p.28.
16. 'A Summer Day', p.27.

You always kept the faith of Wei-sheng,
Who waited under the bridge, unafraid of death,
I never knew I was to climb the Hill of Wang-fu
And watch for you these many days.

I was sixteen when you went on a long journey,
Traveling beyond the Keu-Tang Gorge,
Where the giant rocks heap up the swift river,
And the rapids are not passable in May.
Did you hear the monkeys wailing
Up on the skyey height of the crags?
Do you know your foot-marks by our gate are old,
And each and every one is filled up with green moss?

The mosses are too deep for me to sweep away;
And already in the autumn wind the leaves are falling.
The yellow butterflies of October
Flutter in pairs over the grass of the west garden.
My heart aches at seeing them....
I sit sorrowing alone, and alas!
The vermilion of my face is fading.

Some day, when you return down the river,
If you will write me a letter beforehand,
I will come to meet you — the way is not long
I will come as far as the Long Wind Beach instantly.[17]

---

17. 'Two Letters from Chang-kan' — I, *ibid.*, pp.151-2. I have given
    Obata's complete text here. In Tagore's sensitive but free translation,
    the poem has been shortened by ten lines. Ezra Pound's translation
    ('The River-merchant's Wife: a Letter'), also shorter than Obata's,
    is in *The New Poetry*, but I don't think Tagore used it.

In this poem there is not the slightest sentimentalism; and it carries, so far as I can see, no sidelong glance of mockery or cynicism. The subject-matter is extremely familiar, but there is no lack of emotion in it.[18] If one twisted the style and made it satirical, then it would become 'modern'. This is because modernists despise everything in poetry that everyone else accepts readily. A modern poet would very likely write in the conclusion of the poem that no sooner has the husband departed, rubbing tears from his eyes and looking back frequently, than the girl immediately begins to fry dried prawn dumplings. For whom? In answer to this question there would just be a line-and-a-half of dots. The old-fashioned reader would ask, 'What's going on?' Today's poet would reply, 'This is what often happens.' 'The opposite can happen too.' 'True, but that's much too respectable. If there's no nasty smell, the poem will remain too genteel — it won't be modern enough.' Refinement in old-fashioned poetry had a lot to do with gentility. Today's poetry has its own refinement: in its indulgence of rotten meat!

Alongside the Chinese poem, the modernity of poets in the West is difficult to grasp. It is murky. Their outlook jolts and shoves the reader. The world they are seeing and showing is ramshackle, rubbish-strewn, dust-blown. Their hearts are unhealthy, sick, deranged. In this state of mind, they cannot disengage themselves, in a pure manner, from the mundane world. They roar with laughter at the wood and straw of a broken idol; they say its real character has at last been exposed. These brickbats, this

---

18. *rasa* is used here: the emotion or feeling conveyed by a work of art. The word also means 'juice'.

jabbing at wood and straw with barbed comments, they regard as a strong assertion of the actual truth.

In this context a poem by Eliot comes back to me. It goes like this. An old woman has died — she is from a wealthy family. As is customary, the shutters are closed; the undertakers have arrived and are making appropriate arrangements. Meanwhile, in the dining-room, the footman sits on the edge of the dinner-table, and pulls the second housemaid on to his knee.[19]

No doubt this is a plausible, normal occurrence. But in the mind of a person of an old-fashioned temperament, the question arises: Is this sufficient? What need was there to write this poem? Why should I bother to read it? If I read about a girl's beautiful smile in a poet's composition, I say that this is indeed news worth giving; but if after that I read that a dentist has come, and has discovered with his equipment that her teeth are rotten, I have to agree that this too qualifies as news, but I also say that it's not worth drawing attention to. If I see that someone is especially eager to spread this fact, I suspect that mentally he is rotten himself. If it is claimed that poets in the past wrote selectively, and that ultra-modern poets do not select, I disagree. They select too. To choose a fresh flower is selection, and to choose a dried-up, worm-eaten flower is selection as well. The only difference is that the modernists are forever scared that someone might slander them by saying they have a penchant for selection. There are Tantrics who deliberately eat or handle disgusting things, in case anyone should think that they are partial to pleasant things. The result of this is, they become thoroughly partial to unpleasant things! If in poetry this kind of Tantric practice becomes normal,

---

19. 'Aunt Helen' in *Prufrock and Other Observations* (1917).

then where will those who have a natural taste for wholesome things go? Worms attack certain varieties of tree or flower or leaf, and ignore many others. Should one give priority to the former and boast that this is realism?

A poet has described a respectable gentleman in this way:

Whenever Richard Cory went down town,
    We people on the pavement looked at him:
He was a gentleman from sole to crown,
    Clean favored, and imperially slim.

And he was always quietly arrayed,
    And he was always human when he talked;
But still he fluttered pulses when he said,
    'Good morning,' and he glittered when he walked.

And he was rich — yes, richer than a king,
    And admirably schooled in every grace:
In fine, we thought that he was everything
    To make us wish that we were in his place.

So on we worked, and waited for the light,
    And went without the meat, and cursed the bread;
And Richard Cory, one calm summer night,
    Went home and put a bullet through his head.[20]

---

20. 'Richard Cory' by Edwin Arlington Robinson (1869-1935); from *The New Poetry*. Tagore adds a footnote saying: 'Because I don't have the original poem to hand, I had to translate it from memory — so it might not be quite accurate.' In fact, his translation — in free, not rhymed verse — is almost word-perfect. 'Summer night' has been changed to 'spring night', but that is no doubt because summer would seem less pleasant to Indian readers than spring. It has to be on a pleasant night that Richard Cory shoots himself.

In this poem there is no kind of modernist mockery or ridicule; rather an element of compassion. But there is also a moral, and it is a modern moral. It is this: that what appears outwardly to be healthy and handsome may somewhere harbour a terrible disease within. He whom one thinks is rich may, behind the curtain, be starving. Those who were ascetics of the old sort have spoken in the same terms. They reminded the living: 'One day you will have to ride on a bamboo bier to the cremation-ground.' European enthusiasts for asceticism have described how maggots eat the putrifying, buried body. That the body we think is beautiful is just an ugly assemblage of bone and meat and blood and juice: efforts to remind us of this fact — to shake us out of our complacency — can be found in moralist texts. The best way to encourage ascetic endeavour is to arouse again and again this kind of contempt for appearances. The poet, surely, is not the ascetic's disciple; he follows the path of love. But is this modern age so sickly, that a wind from the cremation-ground is affecting even him? And has he begun to say happily, that what we think to be great is worm-eaten, that in what we cherish as beautiful there is something untouchable?

A mind that has grown old has no strength of pure, natural feeling in it. It has become unhealthy and impure. It tries to dispel its own sluggishness by following a perverse path; it stirs itself up with every kind of ugliness — frothing, fermenting and rotten. Smiles can emerge from its lines and wrinkles only when it abandons shame and revulsion.

The mid-Victorian age wanted to pay reverent homage to reality by treating it with respect; the present age has adopted as its goal the sweeping away of all decorum by insulting what is real.

Appendix B

If one calls excessive reverence for the external world sentimentalism, then one can apply the same name to dogmatic hostility to the world. If, for whatever reason, the mind becomes uncontrolled like this, then vision is no longer clear. So if one ridicules the mid-Victorian age for peddling excessive gentility, one should also ridicule the Edwardian age for possessing the opposite attribute. Its attitude is not natural, so it cannot last for ever. Whether in science or in art, the detached mind is the best vehicle; that which Europe has achieved in science, but not in literature.

Appendix C

A gift of *Āmsattva.*

Mr Sujoy Gupta of Calcutta has kindly given me a hitherto unpublished version of a delightful little poem written by Tagore in thanks for a gift of *āmsattva* — a popular Bengali sweetmeat made from crystallised mango juice. A less polished version of the poem (perhaps a draft) has been printed in *Sphuliṅga 2,* an appendix to Vol. 15 of the West Bengal Government edition of Tagore's collected works (1994) that brings together 299 uncollected short poems. I have said in my Introduction (p.21) that I do not believe the majority of these poems belong with the original *Sphuliṅga* (1945), since they are mostly specific to an occasion or person. But that is not to detract from the charm of a poem such as this.

It was written for Nirupama Devi (1894-1984), Mr Gupta's great aunt by marriage, the wife of the Gandhian freedom-fighter S. K. (Sisir Kumar) Sen, younger brother of Mr Gupta's father's mother. Nirupama was the daughter of a civil servant, and renowned for her beauty. She was first married to the younger son of the Maharaja of Cooch-Behar. When the marriage foundered, she turned to Tagore for comfort, and went to live at Santiniketan. Her second husband, who was the same age as her, had seemed like a confirmed bachelor when they married in their early forties. They had no children. In 1942 they moved to the Madhusudanpur Ashram at Diamond Harbour, and performed heroic social service during the Great Bengal Famine of 1943. They later set up an Ashram of their own at Shahebnagar, near Plassey, and lived there till the end of their lives.

Nirupama was herself a poet, and published three books of poems. From 1923 to 1931 she edited the journal *Paricārikā*. She taught at Santiniketan in the 1920s, and turned several of Tagore's short stories into plays.

Mr Gupta's notebook records that she sent the following poem of her own with the gift of *āmsattva*:

গাছ দিয়েছিল ফল
    ভরা সুমধুর রস
রূপান্তরিত করেছি তাহারে
    এতে নাই হাতযশ !
যতুটুকু এর দাম
    প্রাণের অমৃত দিয়া
তোমার সেবার কারণে হৃদয়

উঠেছিল ব্যাকুলিয়া !
রসনার মধু রসে
      পেয়েছ কি তার স্বাদ ?
রসঘন দুটি ছন্দে তোমার
      দিও মোরে সংবাদ ?

(*gāch diyechila phal*
      bharā sumadhur ras
rūpāntarita karechi tāhāre
      ete nāi hāt-yaś!
yataṭuku er dām
      prāṇer amṛta diyā
tomār sebār kāraṇe hṛday
      uṭhechila byākuliyā!
rasanār madhu rase
      peyecha ki tār svād?
ras-ghana duṭi chande tomār
      dio more sambād?)

The tree gave the fruit,
      Full of sweet juice:
I've merely transmuted it,
      With no great finesse!
What little I did,
      With my own life's nectar,
Was done to serve you
      With heartfelt fervour!

Have you savoured its taste
      With your tongue's sweet juice?
Do tell me with a snatch
      Of your succulent verse!

Here is Tagore's reply:

কল্যানীয়াসু

পাঠালে এ যে আমসত্ত্ব,
সূখ্ম জানি তার তত্ত্ব,
শুধু কি তাহে আমেরি রস রহে ?
যতন করি কোমল হাতে
মিশায়ে দিলে তাহারি সাথে
সে সুধারস দৃশ্য যাহা নহে ।
তাই তো আমি পাই
বাহিরে যাহা নাই,
রসনা যবে তৃপ্ত হয়ে রস চয়নে রতা
অন্তরেতে প্রবেশ করে অরূপ মধুরতা ।

ইতি ২/৭/৩৯   স্নেহাসক্ত
                        রবীন্দ্রনাথ ঠাকুর

(*kalyānīyāsu*

pāthāle e ye āmsattva,
sūkhma jāni tār tattva,
sudhu ki tāhe āmeri ras rahe?

yatan kari komal hāte
misāye dile tāhāri sāthe
se sudhāras dr̥śya yāhā nahe.
tāi to āmi pāi
bāhire yāhā nāi,
rasanā yabe tr̥pta haye ras cayane ratā
antarete prabeś kare arūp madhuratā.

iti 2/7/39   *snehāsakta*
                         Rabīndranāth Ṭhākur)

Dear friend:

This *āmsattva* you've sent -
I know its subtlety:
Is mango juice its only ingredient?
There's a nectar, mixed in carefully,
That your soft hands impart,
That is not so visible:
It cannot be seen externally
But I taste it nonetheless:
While my tongue happily harvests delicious juice,
A sweetness that is not so tangible
Steals into my heart.

Yours affectionately,
Rabindranath Tagore
2.7.39

Nirupama Devi is remembered as one of 'the old Santiniketanites'. She and Tagore and their families were very close. He was very pleased at her second marriage. She used to sing *Rabīndrasaṅgīt* (Tagore's songs) to him. Their mutual affection shines out in these two poems.